P

"It's not often one finds humor, addiction, grief, and genuine openness tangled into one memoir, but L.L. Kirchner's *Blissful Thinking* does exactly that. Traversing both the globe and her inner landscape, Kirchner shows readers what it means to search, try, and even hope during life's most challenging moments."
—Rev. Dr. Angela Yarber, author of *Queering the American Dream*

"A vivid, sharply humorous and insightful account of the pursuit of wellness – L.L. takes you on a trip you'll remember.
—Vasudha Viswanath, author of *The Vegetarian Reset* and Founder, We Ate Well

"This memorable book will send you on a hunt for more of everything inside: more information on yoga, meditation, chanting, gurus, and all the ways these spiritual pursuits do and don't work. In a fascinating travelogue that spans New York City, Qatar, and cities all over India, Kirchner shares the story of her quest for self-improvement. It is told with rich sensory detail, the local food and physical settings in all these locations dropping us right into the moment, with Kirchner's introspection and memories gently pulling us up and out and then back in. There is much to love and learn from all of her attempts at spiritual growth, but her healthy skepticism and strong inner voice is what finally brings her home."
—Debi Lewis, author of *Kitchen Medicine*

BLISSFUL THINKING

A Memoir of Overcoming the Wellness Revolution

BLISSFUL THINKING

A Memoir of Overcoming the Wellness Revolution

L.L. KIRCHNER

OTHER BOOKS BY
L.L. KIRCHNER

*American Lady Creature: (My) Change
in the Middle East*

Text copyright © 2023 by L.L. Kirchner
All Rights Reserved. Printed in the United States of America

Published by Motina Books, LLC, Van Alstyne, Texas
www.MotinaBooks.com

Library of Congress Cataloging-in-Publication Data:
Names: Kirchner, L.L.
Title: Blissful Thinking: A Memoir of Overcoming the Wellness Revolution
Description: First Edition. | Van Alstyne: Motina Books, 2023

Identifiers:

LCCN: 9798887840154

ISBN-13: 979-8-88784-015-4 (paperback)
ISBN-13: 979-8-88784-014-7 (e-book)
ISBN-13: 979-8-88784-016-1 (hardcover)

Subjects: BISAC:
Biography & Autobiography > Personal Memoirs
Biography & Autobiography > Women

Dedication

For anyone still bound by guilt to toxic family dynamics.
There is a way out of shame.

And for my mother. Always.

AUTHOR'S NOTE

The wellness economy is booming. A five trillion-dollar amalgamation of industries, this sector encompasses everything from health clubs to supplements to meditation cushions. As the daughter of health club owners, I've seen this business evolve dramatically in my lifetime, with one constant—the trade is riddled with charlatans and scammers.

While I have no wish to give a pass to the toxic racketeers who prey on vulnerable people, this book isn't a takedown. Not because investigation isn't merited, but because this is my personal exploration of spiritual healing via wellness communities—what helped, what didn't, and why. Despite the flourishing con artistry, there's much to recommend when it comes to things woo. I'm telling my story to show it's possible to benefit from the world of well-being and stay grounded in reality, and I had to develop the skills to do this from an early age.

Growing up, I saw more of Earl Mindell's *Vitamin Bible* than the good book itself, though Mom, my sister and I all watched in horror as Dad sprinkled bran flakes on his nightly salad. When I was twelve, my father quit his corporate job in steel to buy a health club, then demanded that everyone in the family—my reluctant mother included—start working. From there I watched every fad—leg warmers! Herbalife! colloidal silver!—come and go.

My resentment of the family business notwithstanding, I didn't turn *anti*-wellness. I'd rather drink water, take a nap, or get a massage than take aspirin. But I'll take aspirin. And talk therapy vis-à-vis the wellness cult that is 12-Step recovery keeps my substance use disorder in check. Hell, I still work in wellness.

That said, I'm a skeptic by nature. The journalist in me loves a fact check. I'm also a control enthusiast who loves to plan for the next worst thing that could happen. Not that I'm a prepper. All of which is to say—I never planned to write this book.

I didn't realize I was on this quest until it was well underway, though I was writing about my wellness odysseys. After publishing a well-received essay about my first silent meditation retreat, I began writing a book about how meditation healed me. But the story wasn't done cooking.

My crusade turned into an addictive hamster wheel until—after discovering a study from Brown University cataloging the adverse effects vipassana meditation could have—I realized that sitting in silence wasn't what saved me. I trashed that first book to write this story, about discovering bone-deep healing beyond my thinking mind. This tale isn't offered as a one-size-fits-all wellness solution, but to encourage experimentation with the tools of personal growth. Such discovery, I believe, is essential to a full-hearted life.

The privileges inherent in my story—that I'm white and without children and so able to travel—go largely unmentioned within the text unless related to my quest. Personally, I find it jarring when I sense attempts to ward off potential criticism within a narrative. Perhaps it's the wiser approach, but when my heart was breaking and I thrashed in the dark, my driving concern was pain relief. To suggest otherwise feels self-serving.

Most importantly, this is a work of creative nonfiction. My experiences have been recreated through my journals, a blog archive, photographs, calendar entries, and interviews with friends. I've done all I can to be truthful, but blind spots, admiration, and confirmation bias shade memories. Altered and compressed timelines and characters aside, as well as seven years and three significant rewrites in the making, herein lies the truth. I wrote this book to show that it is possible to quit the Sisyphean world of self-help but keep progressing.

INTRODUCTION

Goa, 2011

A crescent moon winked over fairy lights strung amid palm trees. The sand was dotted with friends and beneath it all, a chill lounge soundtrack thrummed in tune with the waves lapping at the Goan shore. The night was perfect, but I was a mess. The clock was closing in on my much-anticipated midnight rendezvous.

Did we say midnight?

Though I had neither a watch nor the kind of phone you checked for time—just a cheap burner with an orange and black screen—I wasn't worried about tardiness. It was New Year's Eve and the countdown to twelve hadn't yet begun. Still, my date was nowhere to be found.

We'd met at yoga while I was in an admittedly vulnerable state. As I'd told my best friend Willy, "I don't think there's a good word for the feeling in English." We were Skyping; Willy was in New York. "In Sanskrit it's

4

called *utkantha,* a longing for lost love."

"Oh please. You don't want that old husband back. You never talk about him anymore."

Didn't Willy know that what I wanted and what I allowed myself to speak of were two different things? Part of me was pleased to be pulling off my charade, yet I was also disappointed Willy didn't know I was faking. But why would he? It had been five years since my divorce, and I'd only been married for four and a half. My right to grieve had expired, only no one had told my heart.

Divorce tore my life into a before, and an after. Willy had only known me after, as my drug and alcohol addiction recovery mentor, or sponsor in the parlance of 12-Step groups. He would've been more in tune with the fact that I'd landed in rehab at nineteen, lost my first love to drowning when I was twenty-four, then returned to actively destructive addiction for years before sobering up again. In light of my addiction catastrophes, my subsequent marriage and divorce might seem trivial. Yet I was consumed by the question, *What is so wrong with me that my other half had to run away?*

Then I met my Yogi Bear.

Blond-haired, blue-eyed, and thick around the middle, YB wasn't my usual type. I hoped that was a positive. "If it's hysterical, it's historical," Willy often said of intense attraction, meaning it was a sign of unresolved family trauma. YB aroused no such concern either at yoga where we met or the house party where we first got to talking.

"Where'd you get the water bottle?" I asked, sincerely not trying to pick the guy up. Parties in Goa weren't geared toward sober attendees and rarely featured nonalcoholic beverages. Tap water was out of the question.

"I brought it with me." He grinned. "I don't drink or do drugs, and I've got caught out at these soirées before."

Drinking or not, most everyone was on *some*thing; I'd assumed YB was too. With this new information, the man before me transformed. His eyes sparkled, his Cockney accent turned hot, and his tattoo sleeves beckoned me to trace their outlines. More compelling still—unlike the vast majority of men I'd met at yoga in India—YB was somewhere close to forty, like me.

Moving to a pile of pillows, we continued our chat. After sharing where he grew up and what he did in his real life, YB broke the news.

"When I get done here, I plan to move to Dubai to teach English."

Dubai as in the Persian Gulf? The place I'd been living when my husband decided to hop a plane and then tell me our marriage was over?

I blinked.

"What're you thinking?" he asked.

"That we should kiss."

This wasn't exactly a lie. I wasn't repulsed by YB— that *is* fatal—I just wasn't super into him. But I wasn't about to let him slip away, not now. If I'd learned anything from looking for love in my forties it was that an age-appropriate guy who practiced yoga in Goa and was clean was a goddamn magical unicorn.

"I want to wait," I'd told him, mid-smooch, not wanting to rush this exploration.

Eventually we'd decided on this night. New Year's Eve. I felt wildly self-possessed even though it was already mid-December.

"Ten!" I heard the countdown begin and scanned the beach.

Where *is* that Yogi Bear?

"Nine!" I looked back toward the patio behind the house, overflowing with partygoers.

Oh, there he is.

"Eight!"

With… a woman?

"Seven!"

Oh. My. God. He is KISSING that woman. Who IS that woman?

"Six!"

Blood filled my ears and the world went dull.

"Five!"

There's nothing wrong with me. It IS me. I AM the problem. I will always be alone.

"Four!"

Tears welled in my eyes. My chest seized. Good gods, don't start crying in the middle of this fucking party.

"Three!"

A flash of movement pulled my gaze from YB. It was Annie, one of the yoga teachers. Spotting me, she smiled broadly and waved me toward where she was dancing on the patio, snapping me back to reality.

We had no history, YB and I. It had been mere weeks since we'd first clapped eyes on each other. Did I care if he was making out with some other chick? If I'd wanted to bang him, I would have. Could I not, for once, enjoy a moment surrounded by friends without replaying my misery or tunneling ahead to my uncertain future?

I could. I would.

Asking why my other half ran away had already taken me down "alternative" healing rabbit holes of tapping, chanting, and energy therapy, to say nothing of my sexual exploits. Still, I remained without a partner to call my own. I feared prospects saw whatever it was that my former other half had unearthed. And it repelled them. I desperately wanted to know what *it* was.

Be crumbled.
So wild flowers will come up where you are.
You have been stony for too many years.
Try something different.
Surrender.
—Rumi

SHOULD I STAY OR SHOULD I GO?

Doha, 2006

My finger hovered over the send button, hesitating. India was but a hazy idea, while the characters on the monitor in front of me were very real.

Was I about to quit the job I'd created out of nothing? The job I'd taken in the relatively safe and centrally-located Persian Gulf country of Qatar to jumpstart my husband's foreign correspondence career? The job that was supposed to establish the nest egg we needed to start a family?

Or was I cutting the cord before they fired me?

Throughout the two and a half years I'd worked at the university I hadn't felt secure in the post or up to its demands. Especially in the last seven months, ever since my husband had abruptly ended our marriage.

Ex-*husband, Lisa*, I reminded myself.

Pushing back from my monitor, I reread my email from the top. Hands in my lap.

```
It is with regret that I write
to inform you of my decision
to resign, effective November 1.
```

That gave my employers six weeks, hardly screwing them over. I'd been trying to quit since just after Valentine's Day, when my beloved had first mentioned wanting to end our marriage. Over the phone. From another country.

While he was at work.

Soon afterward, I'd gone to my boss Robbie to tell her I wanted to leave Qatar. I had no plan, only knew that the prospect of being single and childless in a culture that valued women primarily as wives and mothers was more than I could bear.

"I don't want to turn forty, alone in Doha," I'd said, seeing that September date as outlandishly far into the future.

"I can't blame you," Robbie had said, astounding me with her candor. "I could never live in Qatar."

I felt seen. So far the only person I'd told about my impending divorce was my therapist. My employee benefits (like the house I lived in) were directly tied to my marital status. How much more could I stand losing?

Had I been less shellshocked, I might've proceeded to resign. Starved for positive reinforcement as I was, however, I fell into a hopeful silence, awaiting more validation that my situation was indeed a nightmare.

But Robbie had moved on.

"We're about to start a capital campaign," she said, leaving me to contemplate my foreign landscape alone. What about my marriage? My sacrifices? The patriarchy?

"Until our fundraising efforts are stabilized, how about we keep your departure date flexible?"

She needed me!

Robbie was nodding now, the edge of her wedge haircut swishing as she grabbed me a tissue. It felt so good to feel wanted I'd begun crying.

A couple of months passed before it dawned on me that all my boss had done was prioritize her well-being over mine. I wasn't essential, I was disposable. After realizing this implication, I stewed a few months more.

As I composed my resignation, a full seven months had elapsed and the university had yet to begin searching for my replacement. Mostly, I'd spent that time dithering. Should I stay or should I go?

```
This decision has not come
easily but is one I have
decided to take in light of the
end of my marriage.
```

Sending this missive to my boss and copying all Qatar staff was a passive-aggressive move designed to circumvent further delay. More pointedly, if I didn't say why I was leaving, the rumors would fly.

"Where's your husband?" I imagined my colleagues, associates, and nosy acquaintances asking, innocently or not, once they'd heard I was leaving.

"I don't know," I would've answered. Even in my fantasies I couldn't fathom saying we were divorced, as if I'd had some agency in the decision. Nor could I picture admitting that my other half had left me.

"What happened?" they would've asked.

But I had no way to explain what I didn't understand. What had happened?

At the time, I had more than twenty years into substance recovery, therapy, and general self-examination. How had the ex managed to blindside me? And what the hell else was I missing?

When these conundrums didn't leave me face down or screaming into a pillow, they sent me scurrying to Google. I was going to need a roadmap to escape Qatar, but plans refused to gel.

As the partner responsible for the mortgage back home, I'd put my first efforts into finding gainful employment. From the very office desk where I was editing my farewell, I'd interviewed for a job via Skype with a company in San Francisco. When they asked why I might be the best candidate for their marketing job, however, I'd answered honestly. "I'm not sure I am."

I was in no shape to plot my best life.

Returning to Pittsburgh—where I owned that mortgaged home and my parents lived—felt equally out of the question. I didn't have a job there either, and worse, I could picture similar interrogations, only with friends and family members asking the questions.

"I thought you two were great together," I imagined friends commenting. "What happened?"

Then there would've been my mother's inquisition to face: "WHAT DID YOU DO?"

My fantasies turned toward grad school.

Since first traveling to the Persian Gulf for my then-client, Carnegie Mellon University, I'd wanted to write about the cognitive dissonance that was Qatar, where women wrapped head-to-toe in black floated past Victoria's Secret ads at the mall. But I couldn't summon the will to get transcripts and teacher recommendations, let alone figure out what to study or where.

"Keep doing what you've been doing and you'll get what you've always gotten," I heard. A recovery maxim, I called upon it now to remind myself that these machinations had led me to this moment.

Swiveling in my chair, I faced the credenza behind me. Laden with photographs of friends and travels, I reached into its middle for the snap of my husband and me, all smiles on a Bahamian beach immediately after we'd eloped. Though I'd stopped wearing my wedding ring, I'd kept that picture on display. For others to see. Plucking the frame from the shelf, I tossed the thing into the garbage and turned back to my letter.

```
I will miss the many wonderful
colleagues I've had the honor
of working with.
```

Given the first year I'd had on campus, the sincerity of this line took me aback.

When the university had first announced it was opening a Doha branch, plans did not include a communications department. Given the extraordinary wealth in the Persian Gulf, this oversight struck me as a wasted opportunity. Around that same time, my husband's newspaper disclosed it was folding, and Qatar's Al Jazeera revealed they were opening an English-language outlet. If I could nab a three-year contract with the university, we'd be financially set to return home and start a family. So I drew up an ambitious marketing proposal.

Of the many schemes I plotted in innocence, one of my more colossal missteps was underestimating the difficulty of employee recruitment. It took more than a year to find an administrative assistant, meanwhile the enormous task list I'd created to justify my position fell squarely on me. Coupled with the eight-hour time difference between Doha and the main campus, working overtime was a daily occurrence that left little time for friends or family. My physical and mental health were pushed to the brink, and my husband and I devised a new plan—he would return to the States to look for work, and as soon as he found a job I would join him.

Or that's what I thought we'd decided before that intercontinental divorce phone call.

`I'm delighted to share that I'll be—`

Delighted? That was a bit of an overstatement for the plan I'd arrived at.

Between what I had in savings and renting out my house in the States, I could last about six months in any number of countries that offered long-term visas, a breather I desperately needed. Yet the apparent preponderance of choice was deceiving once I started digging into my options.

Classic extended-travel jaunts—such as trekking in Nepal or any other opium-exporting paradise—seemed like asking to slide back down the shame spiral of drugs and alcohol, which I wouldn't endure. And this was the heart of my dilemma.

In the past, lost love had led me to drug and alcohol relapse. I felt as low now as I had when I'd returned to my addictions. In the nine years since reclaiming my sobriety, I'd worked hard at the kind of self-examination a clean and sober life required. That work had neither saved me from the unceremonious dumping, nor had it shielded me from this pain. Would my sobriety hold this time?

Maintaining long-term sobriety was going to require more than merely changing track. I needed to destroy my ignorant self and be reborn a new person. First, I needed a goddamn break. During the respite I envisioned, my mind would clear and my heart would heal, resulting in better relocation planning than I'd done for Qatar. Such scheming required safety and space, twin needs that eliminated the world of volunteer abroad opportunities.

"You're so great with these kids," I fantasized someone saying, because the universe of work abroad situations I qualified for involved children. "When are you going to have your own?"

Having recently learned I'd never have kids, these storylines were as daunting as returning to my former hometown. Then I came across a yoga teacher training in

Goa, India.

Clean living would be supported. Hell, I attempt vegetarianism. And getting a certificate would show that I hadn't been mowed down by pain. Best of all, the course came with a deadline—classes started in one month. I had to act now or risk losing my spot on the course.

But *delighted?* That line needed an edit.

```
I'm pleased to share that I'll
be joining the teacher training
course at the Brahmani Yoga
Shala in Goa, India.
```

Of course I'd never actually be a yoga teacher—I loved cigarettes and hated patchouli—but a couple of months on a beach in Goa sounded like the reprieve I needed. I knew yoga—my parents had owned a gym. What could go wrong?

I looked back at my computer. Watched my cursor blink some more. My resistance reared. I could leave my job and be equally miserable, with the added prize of being broke. My eyes bounced to a curled sticky note dangling at the bottom of my screen, a quote from Pema Chödrön that I'd heard in yoga: "The most difficult times for many of us are the ones we give ourselves."

Taking a deep breath, I dared to hope. Maybe I'd once and for all lose this darkness, this void I'd tried to sate with drugs and alcohol and sex and shopping and sugar. Conjuring all the light I could muster, I pressed send. Then I bolted from my desk for a smoke.

GOA, INDIA

Goa, 2006

The welcome packet from Brahmani Yoga had advised taking two weeks to decompress and mentally prepare before starting the teacher training course, more if you were leaving behind a stressful situation. I'd given myself two days and already my life had transformed.

Beyond the geographic metamorphosis—the time difference between Doha and Anjuna Beach was only two and a half hours—I'd created an entirely new life from scratch, trading my Audi for an Activa scooter, my Palm Pilot for a basic Nokia 3310 (Airtel India credits were cheaper than internet cafés), and heels for flip-flops.

The yoga course was scheduled to start the next day, and though I wasn't entirely sure how to get to the shala, or where to buy groceries, I'd happily detoured to Ravi's condo.

We stood in a bright, modern kitchen—a stark contrast to the rustic guesthouse I'd rented. I leaned on the island while Ravi propped against the sink.

"You're sure it's cool if I stay here?" I asked. My potential new landlord had deep brown eyes rimmed with thick lashes, a sexy British accent, and latté-colored skin coating what looked like a yogi's body. Only, Ravi wasn't a yoga guy. We'd just met in a 12-Step meeting I'd managed to find.

Ravi smiled and my heart leapt. He wouldn't be the first man I'd slept with since my husband left. That distinction went to a colleague with a fetching, gap-toothed smile, a man who'd dumped me as soon as his real girlfriend came back in the picture. But maybe the recovery bond Ravi and I shared would enable deeper connection.

"This is my parents' place, but they're staying in London this season," he said. "They think my girlfriend will be staying here. She doesn't arrive for a couple of weeks, and anyway, she'll stay with me. My place is just a few doors over."

My main takeaway there was, of *course* he has a girlfriend.

"You can stay for free."

I was happy enough in the guest house, but free was hard to turn down. Besides, my current lodging was only short-term. The condo was available for the full length of my stay. Plus, it came with a pool.

"I'd love to, thank you," I said, hoping my disappointment hadn't shown.

"How about a coffee?" His accent was far more compelling than the thought of caffeine, not that I needed to be particularly alert the next morning.

"Sure." Yoga started early the next day, but it was *yoga*. Not an exam. This trip was basically an extended holiday. What was one more paper cut of dismissal? Cute as Ravi was, and attractive as this rooming situation might be, I'd followed him home because of something he'd said in the meeting.

"What did you mean when you said everything changed when you learned how to break free of emotional dependency?"

"That's my S.L.A.A. talking," he said, pronouncing the acronym as individual letters.

"S.L.A.A.?"

"Sex and Love Addicts Anonymous," he said, handing me a chipped mug.

I froze. Sex addict? Maybe I shouldn't stay here.

"Don't panic, love."

I looked into my mug, where I couldn't help but notice its ceramic edge was stained. Was it dirty, or was something dark indelibly etched into the cup?

"That's where I get most of my recovery these days," Ravi said. "I'm a love addict through and through."

I smiled, trying to cover my obvious relief. I didn't know what a love addict was exactly, only that it conjured something far less disturbing than sex addict. "Is that so bad?"

"It was for me," he said, turning serious. "I had to learn to stop hiding from other people but maintain my boundaries. Emotional sobriety. Surely by now you know that's key to staying clean long-term."

Since sharing sobriety dates had been part of the

meeting, Ravi knew I'd been sober almost a decade and I was aware that he had twelve continuous years. Though technically he had more clean time, I'd been going to meetings far longer. Even so, I'd never heard the phrase "emotional sobriety."

"I know I can't handle misery," I said, matching his deliberate tone. "I met my first real boyfriend in rehab. I was a patient, but Jeffrey was a volunteer. That's not cool, I know. But we waited till I had three months. And he was there for me all through those early years of sobriety. He even gave me a job when I graduated from college."

I paused, thinking back to the summer after graduation when I worked for Jeffrey's painting business. Failing to land a job in journalism had turned me tragically morose, and I'd cried over my presumed wasted future daily. Antidepressant medication was discouraged in recovery back then. Fortunately, the clouds lifted when I got my first professional job. For a few years anyway.

"Then he drowned," I said. "And I was devastated."

"I'm so sorry," Ravi said.

I looked into Ravi's eyes. *All the good ones are taken.*

"It was a long time ago now. But you're right, his death forced me to be more aware of my emotions. Because for a couple of years after he died, I was sober and miserable, which I didn't realize until after I sobered up again. I learned that misery and sobriety did not go together."

What I didn't add was that I felt very much the same now as I had when Jeffrey died, raw at my core, guarded against anything that might chafe the wound.

Ravi was nodding. "Then you know exactly what I mean."

"Mmm," I murmured, a sound something like assent even though I really wasn't sure. Mostly I liked that he didn't ask what most people did: "Was your boyfriend sober when he died?" As if using made sense of the tragedy.

But Jeffrey died with ten years clean. Sobriety hadn't saved him.

That night, while packing up what little I'd brought to India for the move to Ravi's, I came across the red and gold carton of Dunhill cigarettes I'd purchased in Doha's duty-free. The box was still wrapped in cellophane. Had I not had a cigarette in two days? I hadn't even noticed.

As far back as I could remember, I'd been obsessed with smoking. Perhaps I was attracted to the habit because of my glamorous mother, with her razorblade cheekbones, leopard print tops, and bright red lips that left kisses on the ends of her cigarettes. But I attribute my early fascination with smoking—and even booze—to the old black and white movies we used to watch together. The broads in those films could command a room with their witty repartée, cocktail in hand, a smoke dangling from their lips. They were the epitome of what I was not—authoritative, independent, urbane.

My mother didn't encourage that vision so much as discourage me from staying in the Rust Belt suburbs where we lived. "We're in hell," she once complained. "Without the amenity of a sidewalk."

Whenever possible, Mom mentioned that she and my father were from Chicago. Shortly after my sister was born, however, they'd begun moving from one bedroom community to the next. By the time I was twelve, she and my father had moved eleven times. Though occasionally local, most moves were major cultural and climactic upheavals. Illinois to Maryland to Massachusetts to Pennsylvania to Michigan to Alabama and back to Pennsylvania. This wasn't normal for metallurgical engineers, but my dad was ahead of his time when it came to his career trajectory. Mom must've been lonely. Sometimes she'd fail to question an illness I fcigned, I'd stay home from school, and we'd spend the day watching old movies on TV.

I was ten the first time I smoked for real. It wasn't my first attempt but the time I learned to inhale. Though I'd never smoked more than, at most, half a pack a day, I couldn't quit. In the ensuing thirty years I'd tried repeatedly, using pills, patches, gum, and sometimes all three at once. But I never quit and thought, *So that's what food tastes like!* My experience was more like, *That lady on the opposite side of the highway is smoking, why can't I?*

Yet there I was in India where, by merely landing, the desire to smoke had vanished. Pulling the carton to my nose, I inhaled the rich tobacco scent oozing out of the plastic. Though I still had no interest in smoking one, I tucked the carton into my luggage. Best to hold onto those Dunhills for when this bonkers miracle came to an end and the urge to smoke returned. Far better, for an addict like me, to smoke a cigarette instead of a joint.

It took mere days for Ravi's parents to discover the ruse. I had to find another guesthouse. Having to move unexpectedly was jarring. In my twenties, a boyfriend had called me a "rootless cosmopolitan," which I thought sounded cool until my thirties came and went and I began to feel anxious about my lack of constancy.

"To know who you are," Carson McCullers once wrote, "you have to have a place to come from."

Though I couldn't change the fact that I came from nowhere, I could establish a home. So far, however, I wasn't lolling on Anjuna's beaches like I'd imagined, contemplating my options. Between pre-dawn morning practices, assistant teaching, afternoon classes, and evening meditation sessions, I hadn't even used Ravi's pool.

I took one final sweep of the condo to be sure I wasn't leaving anything behind and spotted my yoga mat standing guard by the door. *That's less surprising than it should be,* I thought.

Picking up the extra thick mat I'd brought from Qatar, I folded it to lay atop my scooter's seat, locked the door, and left the keys under the doormat. Disappointed as I'd been to lose this spot, I'd lucked into a last-minute opening in the compound where most of Brahmani Yoga's teachers lived, a place they called "Big Brother," which was more than a little forbidding.

THE FAILED VEGETARIAN

Goa, 2006

The first difference I noticed at Big Brother was the nocturnal symphony of dogs and chickens and goats and cows. I'd barely slept before my phone's alarm buzzed to life, the sun had yet to stir.

After guzzling two cups of black tea to rouse myself, I didn't have much to do besides slip into my Lycra gym gear. I'd taken my cold-water bucket shower the night before. Slinging my canvas book bag over my shoulder, I stepped outside, only to scurry back into my room. Between the slightly earlier start (the shala had been much closer to Ravi's), the fact that December was creeping closer, and the years I'd spent in the Persian Gulf, I couldn't handle the chill. By the time I'd swathed myself in enough scarves to stay warm, I looked like a proper Ibiza hippie taking off into the dark stillness, my breath visible in the air.

The yoga shala consisted of a small hut next to a cement pad, a space protected from the great outdoors with a wrap of mosquito netting. Each day, we convened there for roughly two hours, the length of time it took to go through our individual yoga practices. Afterward, we took yoga class with Jenny, the head of the program.

Once the people in Jenny's class who weren't on the training course had cleared out, we'd spend another couple of hours on that slab, learning anatomy, postures, and adjustments. After breaking for lunch, we either took or assisted with more classes. In the evening, we spent another couple of hours crouched on that same floor, studying yoga philosophy and meditating.

On the second night of this grueling schedule, we gathered for a welcome dinner. Including the teachers, there were about fifteen of us. Over a shared platter of hummus—which I had to refrain from devouring in its entirety—we introduced ourselves, and the head teacher explained her philosophy.

"You must know the physical, mental, and practical aspects of what it takes to make a living teaching yoga. And if you're to study with me," Jenny said. "You must learn the spiritual elements that inform the practice. And you must be willing to let those elements inform your life."

In addition to being the only other person near forty within miles, Jenny was also the only other American I'd encountered. When it was time for dialog, I felt comfortable asking the question that—fueled by my gnawing hunger and growing fatigue—had begun to plague me. "Do you lose many people on this course?"

This earned a hard stare from Jenny. I'd noticed that she, like me, had picked up scads of Briticisms. Unlike me, she'd adopted a slight British accent. "Wot d'you mean?"

What did I mean? I could scarcely imagine many people actually succeeded in completing her course. Failing to score the yoga teaching certificate would put a swift end to my fantasy of triumph in the face of pain. I persisted. "I mean, do many people drop out?"

"I've never had anybody drop out," Jenny said with an air of certitude I found daunting. There was a gravity to her, a seriousness borne of introspection that gave off an air of, "Don't fuck with me."

Tweaked as I can be by authority, it took all my will not to respond, "There's a first time for everything."

Big Brother was positioned at the center of the action, with near-nightly parties featuring fire shows, beatboxing, and/or didgeridoos. Yet I felt apart from the action. Adrift. It didn't help that I kept having accidents—I toppled my scooter on three separate occasions, burned my hand severely (mercifully only once), and regularly found mysterious bruises all over my body. Finally my classmate, Debra, took me to lunch and proceeded to order for me.

"A hamburger in India? Debra, are you mad?"

Debra had more than one master's degree, and exuded competence at everything. She'd been living in India for years by the time we met, and had perfected the art of fusion garb—bold shalwar kameez paired with dangly earrings and jeweled kitten heels. I'd gone in the opposite direction—when I wasn't doing yoga, my go-to outfit was a cargo-style mini skirt paired with a rugby shirt. She'd also brought along her husband, and though he wasn't doing the training, he often stumbled his way through a morning practice. *What must that be like?* I often wondered. My ex had never shown any interest in yoga.

"You're not getting enough calories or protein," Debra said, pushing the offending platter toward me. "Eat. Or resign to injuring yourself more."

I looked at the burger, disheartened. Even if I wasn't going to be a teacher, I wanted to be a yogi and, though not a requirement to practice, most all espoused a vegetarian lifestyle. Nonetheless, I took a bite and, much to my dismay, felt better instantly.

So much for choosing yoga, I thought, upbraiding myself for eating meat. A by-product of 1970s suburban America, before moving to Qatar I'd never heard of a yoga *shala*, let alone the type of practice we were learning to teach on Jenny's course—Ashtanga.

Of course I'd done yoga before arriving in Doha, but no one in my family considered stretching a form of exercise. Yoga was something you did between real sports, or when you were injured.

All my life I'd worked out several times a week, whether I wanted to or not. My parents owned a gym. So it wasn't until I started working for the university and slammed into a sedentary routine that I realized my exercise habit was a need. But Qatar's gyms held "ladies" hours, while this lady was at work. The only available option was a yoga class, which I resisted. Until my doctor suggested adding a neck brace to the knee and wrist braces I was already wearing. I had to admit it—I looked like I'd been in a car accident.

I barely made it through my first class. The Doha Sheraton's basketball court was barely visible beneath unfurled yoga mats, but there was no mistaking the occupants. *Work colleagues.*

Was I going to have to huff and puff my way back to fitness in front of the lithe school nurse? The hot IT guy? Christ, even our yoga teacher worked on campus.

Worse yet, in Ashtanga the sequence is a progression. You're only taught a posture once you've mastered the poses leading up to it. This philosophy ensures you're ready for what's to come. Though flexible, I'd never been terribly strong or possessed of deft eye-hand coordination. I had to work for every pose. I certainly never saw myself teaching yoga; I'd never be a skilled enough practitioner to teach. But I'd hoped I might be a yogi.

My fellow students like Debra, on the other hand, were teacher material. Ninjas, all, and young enough to be my children. Oftentimes I felt as if they were. Not in a maternal way, more like my exhaustion made me feel as if I'd just given birth. Not that I had any clue what that might be like. I'd never been pregnant, and never would be.

Back in Qatar I'd begun experiencing chronic insomnia. I blew up over small things, and regularly found myself bathed in sweat, all symptoms I'd attributed to culture shock and workload. I also traveled frequently, constantly straddling time zones. When my period stopped, I viewed the reprieve as a bonus.

"You're in menopause," my gynecologist said at my annual appointment, all terse and British-like. I was gobsmacked.

Finally, something to explain the sweating and the hair trigger rage I'd unknowingly backed into. A physical deficiency I could fix. There was just one outstanding issue.

"The world should have more people like you," I'd said to my other half not long after we'd wed. "But let's wait a couple of years. Get a solid foundation in *us*."

Then the Qatar opportunity came up. The reasonable thing, we'd reckoned, was to hold off on kids until after we'd left the Persian Gulf. That would put me at forty, the same age my nana had given birth to my dad.

All that changed with this diagnosis, a shift I wanted to talk about all the time. But my husband had no such desire. The office, where I spent most of my time, wasn't the place to bring up the issue, especially not in the Muslim world. My friends back home—when I could reach them around the eight-hour time difference—weren't interested in the topic. When I broached the subject, I was greeted with the kind of enthusiasm you might expect for admitting you had some dread, communicable disease. Same with my sister.

My mom was the only woman I knew well who'd been through the change of life, but her willingness to indulge my inquiry amounted to a single sentence. "I didn't have the luxury of symptoms, not with my work schedule."

We should all be so lucky as to live to see menopause, a small voice inside me whispered, but I didn't give it credence. I'd come of age reading Erica Jong and Judith Krantz, I was comfortable mocking the fear of sexuality. But the end of sexuality? I was as afraid of that as anyone.

To my surprise, the last gasp of hormones galloping through my body aroused an urgent libido, unfortunately coinciding with the end of my marriage. Luckily in Qatar, the men outnumbered the women. But the scattered flings did little to quell my needs. So it was an unexpected bonus when the yoga course left me too knackered for lust.

Though disappointed I failed to achieve vegetarianism, had I not continued eating meals that included animal protein, I doubt I'd have finished the course. Along with my certificate, I got an award. We all did. Debra's was "Best Bollywood Style." Mine was "Most Accident Prone."

After our graduation ceremony, I returned to my room at Big Brother and pulled my suitcase out from under my bed to stow my certificate. The carton of Dunhills was still inside. I ran my fingers over the red and gold box's embossed logo, astonished I'd not smoked at all. Not even wanted to. How was that possible?

"The answer is always more spirituality," I heard, a slogan Elaine, a previous sponsor, had been fond of saying.

Given that 12-Step recovery is based on developing a spiritual approach to life, her advice was not unusual. Thinking back on those words now, however, it occurred that I might do well to apply her wisdom. Even my demanding schedule had been no shield—in India, outward expressions of worship were everywhere.

Unlike the stringent Catholicism I'd been raised with, Hinduism, India's majority religion, wasn't a single philosophy but a combination of many different beliefs. Gods are viewed as complementary rather than contrasting. Temples are devoted to Lakshmi and Shiva and Nandi alike. And such displays weren't exclusive to Hindus. From Buddha statues to the shrines of village deities to the marigold-laden crosses I saw in the Christian churches that dotted the landscape, there was no escaping the profusion of gods and goddesses.

Taking a whiff of Dunhill, I wondered if maybe this was what had drawn me here, this holy aspect. Never before had addiction relief been so effortless. If merely showing up could accomplish this miracle, what might happen if I applied myself? At least a little?

Tossing the smokes in the garbage, I noticed a flier I'd thrown away. At a party a few days earlier, I'd watched practitioners giving aquatic massages. "What are they doing?" I'd asked Debra.

"Watsu. It's a rebirthing therapy."

"They're going to need that. It looks like they're drowning." I wasn't joking. Dread struck my heart as I watched, but now I wondered if such a thing would be good for me.

Pressing the paper to my chest, I looked into the garbage can and vowed, if it would help me heal, I would say yes to any spiritual invitation laid before me, no matter how absurd it might seem.

IT WILL CHANGE EVERYTHING

Goa, 2006

Late as I was already, I took the longer route from Anjuna Beach to Ashvem, where I was supposed to meet Debra. Local cops had been stopping traffic at the main intersection out of town, issuing fines to tourists on scooters. I hated being late, but I was counting every rupee. Not that I minded the detour.

Traversing the ribbons of road that ran through the low-lying, non-touristic seaside villages was a treat. I adored following these jungle byways, cry-singing along to what my friend Bubsy had long ago dubbed "cliff music," for making her want to jump from a rocky precipice. But I'd always loved how the raw emotion expressed by musicians like The Stars, Neko Case, and Scrawl had enabled me to purge mine.

When I pulled up, Debra was already eating. Like many structures in Goa, the restaurant was open-air, essentially a covered porch with a thatch roof. When the monsoons came the canopies would be taken down and stored, ready for reconstruction once the rains ended and the tourists returned the following season. There was nothing quite so pleasant as an afternoon whiled away in one of these shady spots.

"I couldn't wait," Debra said, putting down her forkful of salad to stand and hug me. "I was starving after practice today."

Consciously stopping myself from patting her back—a habit of my family's I'd learned was a signal to stop embracing—I wasted no time letting Debra off the hook. "Please. You know better than anyone I'm hypoglycemic. And anyway, I'm the one who should apologize for being late. Traffic stop at Siolim."

I didn't mention the weep-song that had also slowed me considerably. Even after the teacher training, watsu, and a round of panchakarma (a week of juicing and more massage), my baseline state remained "on-the-verge-of-tears." Yet I held out hope. An Ayurvedic doctor had recently prescribed herbs that had quelled my hot flashes and enabled full nights of sleep. Even so, beneath our banter, I couldn't stop the drumbeat of *what are you going to do now?* Was this emotional tar pit my life from here on out?

My curry arrived.

"When do you leave?" Debra asked.

Could she tell I had no plan? "My visa's still good for another month and I want to write about Qatar." Maybe I could borrow from her plan. "I should probably go for an MFA. Where did you go?"

"Well, I have two master's but they're both in science," Debra said, then leaned closer, her emerald Indian tunic heightening the blue in her eyes. "You wanna know what I think?"

More than anything.

Locking me with her gaze she said, "You should try a vipassana." Then she sat back against her chair and stroked her long dark ponytail.

Before this trip, I'd never even heard of a vipassana, let alone imagined myself sitting in silence for ten straight days. Since landing in India, however, I'd heard this suggestion multiple times. But what good would sitting still for ten days do?

"Other people have mentioned that," I said, poking at my curry in an attempt to seem casual. "But how can not talking—"

"Ten days of sitting in silence," Debra interrupted, "and you'll know everything."

She was still stroking her hair. Was she high?

"They say that vipassana helps you replace anger and misery with an unshakeable foundation of love and happiness."

Say what now?

Even before I started doing yoga in Qatar I'd heard of the Inner Buddha concept, a golden essence of pure love supposedly housed at the center of every human being. Our earthly task was to make it shine. Meditation was supposed to help.

When I sat in silence, however, the only core I regularly touched was fury, red and hot. Near as I could tell, my Inner Buddha was a real bitch. And she was pissed.

Hadn't I promised I'd try anything though? I *still* wasn't smoking and, by some miracle, never thought about it except in awe that quitting hadn't been a struggle. Or even an attempt. I should hold up my end of the bargain—which I'd struck with no one—and accept the healing opportunity that had appeared.

"When did you do a vipassana?" These ten-day sits were referred to as a "vipassana," though I'd later learn this was the name of this particular type of meditation. Who knew there were types?

"Me?" Debra had finished her meal and moved on to smoking an enormous spliff, which she put down with a smirk. "Can you imagine me not talking for ten days?" She shook her head and peered into the distance.

Outside this trip I'd avoided being around weed. Pot was what I'd gone back out on initially ("out" as in out of recovery; no longer sober). Even when I didn't feel on the verge of relapse, I found its pungent scent triggering. But not in India. Perhaps it was the fragrant competition—the omnipresent cows, roadside markets heaping with marigolds and spices, the incense smoldering everywhere—but like my nicotine habit, my need to avoid the smell of marijuana had disappeared. This was a boon, given that the tourists lit up everywhere.

"What makes you think *I* could do a vipassana?"

Debra refocused her attention on me, narrowing her glassy eyes. "Maybe you couldn't," she eventually said. "But why not give it a try?"

As I climbed the stairs to the travel agency/internet café later that afternoon, I felt better than usual. Instead of harboring vague hopes I'd hear from the ex, I was on a mission to research vipassana retreats. Was such a place nearby? Would a retreat be starting soon? How much would it cost?

Mission aside, of course I checked my email first and, for once, found delight—an acceptance letter.

While still in Qatar, I'd submitted a flash essay for a Miranda July project called *Learning to Love You More*, a book containing art and words about love. My piece included a hand-drawn rendering of my Motorola Razr alongside a fanciful conversation with my ex. In it, I confront him. In response, my beloved acknowledges his wrongdoings. He doesn't apologize—not even in the wilds of my imagination did I picture that—but he does ask me to take him back. Without hesitation, I agree. The opposite, in every way, to the conversation we did have, which had begun with this email:

We need to talk.

My husband never needed to talk. Though it was midnight my time and 8 a.m. where he was, and I was a morning person and he was a night person, I phoned immediately. Confoundingly he'd taken a "temporary" job at the same alternative newsweekly where he'd been working when we first met. I knew he'd be in the office—it was deadline day.

"Who's this?" asked the receptionist.

Was she cute? "His wife?"

"What's your name?"

If we exchanged any pleasantries, they're lost. All I remember is this: "I want a divorce."

My bones knew this was final but my heart rebelled. My head, awkward as ever, intervened.

"Couldn't we try counseling first? At least fight-ing?"

Neither of us laughed. He said nothing.

Finally, I said the words I never imagined having to say. "I don't want a divorce."

His words left no room for interpretation. "This is not negotiable."

Staring at the monitor in the internet café, replaying— as I often did then—the real conversation with my ex, I recognized two chilling truths. First, I was buoyed that something good had come of my delusion—my first writing to ever appear in a book! Second, as I reread my entry, I knew it was still true. Given the slightest opening, I would take my ex back.

His ongoing hold was not his looks, though I found him terribly handsome—tall, dark-haired, olive-skinned. What kept me bewitched was his most irresistible quality, a sense of ease in the world. I had nothing like that.

Begging results from the café's hulking beast of a computer, I typed with mad urgency: "Vipassana meditation retreat centers."

To my surprise page after page of results appeared. Narrowing to India only, there were still more than a hundred centers. Clicking on the first few results, I discovered they were booked until well past my visa's expiration date. Zeroing in on a map, I found a center outside Bengaluru, the tech hub southwest of Goa in the neighboring state of Karnataka, where Debra lived. They had open spots, but the course started in less than two weeks. Without bothering to read more, I hurriedly clicked on the application.

I didn't make it past the name and address block before slight nausea came over me. Outside the Big Brother compound, I had no address. I went with my parents' house.

Then came the question:

```
"Do you have, or have you ever had,
any mental health problems such as
significant depression or anxiety,
panic attacks, manic depression,
schizophrenia, etc.? If yes, please
give details (dates, symptoms,
duration, hospitalization,
treatment, and present condition)."
```

Obviously, I should lie. Right?

A FRUSTRATING MYTH

Goa, 2007

Beads of sweat formed on my forehead as I pushed into the plastic backing of the internet café's lawn chair style seat. I reread the vipassana center's question on the monitor. Like it would change.

> "Do you have, or have you ever
> had, any mental health problems…"

What if ten days of seated silence required a stamina I didn't possess?

Aware of the little clock counting rupees in the screen's upper right-hand corner, I stared. More sweat pooled on my upper lip and in my armpits. *A hot flash? Now?*

Leaning forward I typed into the search bar, "will my vipassana application be rejected if I've spent time in a mental hospital?"

The results yielded page upon page of non-answers in the form of FAQs promoted by various retreat centers. Of course *they* weren't going to help applicants game the system. I tried new search words.

"Vipassana issues and mental illness."

That search brought up an old blog post written by a self-proclaimed meditation expert.

"Retreats aren't recommended for people with serious psychiatric disorders," he wrote. According to this author, centers also screened for people who did Reiki, though it wasn't clear if he meant people who'd had sessions or offered them or both. Not that the energy massages I'd had were what sent me down this spiral. I was screwed from "any mental health problems." My playlist included multiple institutionalizations, starting when I was a freshman at OSU.

As the rupees mounted, I recalled what that had been like, feeling as though I'd just woken up without knowing where I was. Given the amount of partying I'd been doing, the confusion was common enough, but this time the disorientation felt different. Like those liminal moments before you're asleep and your body shakes to catch itself. Only there was no waking up. No getting out. Time itself had melted.

At last, I asked. "Where am I?"

Narrowing her eyes, the woman I'd addressed paused. She couldn't have been much older than I, a college sophomore. Pursing her lips as if scanning for the appropriate answer, she also asked. "Upham Hall?"

But the name meant nothing. "What's that?"

This time, even more tentatively, "A psychiatric ward?"

Shaking the lint from my brain, I tried to remember a time when I hadn't been in this prison. It was walking across campus.

I'd just bought a dime bag of weed. From my initial sample, the world had begun to come apart. Everything—myself included—dissolved into streaks of light, and we were all being sucked along as if through a vacuum tube. Choice was an illusion.

Rather than share the stash as was customary, I ducked into every dark corner, alley, and isolated toilet stall I could find to pull out my one-hitter. I didn't sleep for days, obsessed as I was with watching the discrete world melt.

On a Walkman—stolen from some rich kid I'd slept with—I played *The Jimi Hendrix Experience* on repeat, certain his words were a message. "Manic depression's a frustrating myth," I belted and walked and ducked.

Slowly I became aware of others on the ward. Vonnie—whose gray hair frizzled to the end—paced the halls day after day, chasing grooves only she could see. She would be the same on my next visit.

Tom came. Tom, the dashing rugby player who left me cold. Him I asked to marry me.

My sister visited and brought a DIY card that read, "When ya coming home?" Looking at it made me cry. I had no idea.

One time I escaped, slipping out as the doors locked behind me. But after riding the elevator down and running out the front doors, I didn't know where to go. I had to knock to be let back in.

By the time I was officially released, the school year had ended. At least I didn't have to face my dormmates. There followed a puffy summer of beer and forgetting meds then doubling up on doses. I got my first driver's license and my first diagnosis—manic depressive.

I looked back at the blog post on the computer monitor. The author was suggesting that, for people with certain mental illnesses, a vipassana could trigger a break with reality. I'd had enough of those.

But am I really mentally ill?

This doubt had persisted for years, no matter how hard I tried to banish it. Continuing to ignore the unspooling clock, I lingered on the ways I'd manipulated my various diagnoses, starting with the very next school year.

By Thanksgiving, I was so desperate to feel cared for, I signed myself into Upham Hall, claiming a depressive state. All I had to do was tell my shrink how I longed to swallow a bottle of pain pills. I doubt I ever told him how I'd gotten my knee injury, how the policeman who'd dropped me trying to break up a fight had ended up waiting for me at the hospital before driving me home to my scholarship dorm.

During my second stay at Upham, I noticed Vonnie was also back. Or still there. This lodged fear in my gut. I did not want to grow up to be like Vonnie, wild-haired and mumbling as I paced between locked corridors.

My diagnosis was amended to bipolar disorder.

By spring quarter of my sophomore year, I stopped sleeping again. I was sure I was heading into a manic phase, but a friend of my mother's corrected me over the phone. "That pot was laced with PCP. You're not mentally ill, you don't have the affect of a mentally ill person. You're an alcoholic."

Though the woman was neither a medical professional nor had she clapped eyes on me in some three years, I wanted to believe her. If there was one thing I knew after a year of living with mental illness it was that I didn't want to live with mental illness. At any moment, my brain could betray me. And so began my addiction recovery.

When I met Jeffrey in rehab, I wouldn't have put us together. My clothes were second-hand and I bought independent-label records for a store called Magnolia Thunderpussy. Jeffrey sported a mullet and listened to Robert Palmer without irony. But he wouldn't quit me.

When my birthday came around the first time, I

hadn't mentioned the big day. When he came to pick me up for dinner, no gift in hand, I pouted. Hadn't he noticed the birthday cards in my room? So what if they competed with the buzzy ephemera of four college girls sharing a space?

Given the communication skills I'd developed between moving and drinking, I figured we were over.

"Relationships aren't faucets, Keesha," Jeffrey said, because that's what he called me. And for the next five years, he showed me what he meant.

When I graduated he gave me the job with his painting company—we were both hoping for more. By the time I got my first professional job in public relations for the Columbus Museum of Art, Jeffrey was teaching scuba. A few years prior we'd watched a TV special about pearl divers in the Persian Gulf, and Jeffrey had been obsessed with diving ever since.

One afternoon he called to see if I wanted to join him at his mom's pool. He wanted to practice his free diving skills, holding breath underwater. But I declined. Work.

That night I got a call from his sister's boyfriend, Mark.

"Jeffrey's dead."

"No, he's—"

"He died at his mom's swimming pool this afternoon."

I have a photograph from that summer, taken at the museum. In it my hair is a dark auburn and my oversized striped shirt is askew; I appear caught off guard, but that was pretty much what I looked like at all times then. My face and eyes are splotched red. I must've been crying somewhere, though I've no recollection, only the picture.

Jeffrey died sober, but as a consequence of his teenage Dilaudid habit. Only twenty-six, his heart gave out. For two years following his death, my thinking grew increasingly compulsive. The journal I kept reveals only what I was willing to commit to the page. My thoughts were another matter.

"People who are addicted to food still have to eat, but they recover. Shouldn't alcohol be the same?"

Not that I'm going to drink.

"No one will ever love me like Jeff did."

I hate myself. I hate myself. I hate myself.

"You can do everything right, and still, your life can suck."

If this is sobriety, fuck it.

But I knew how to muscle through a crisis. The thought of getting psychiatric help never crossed my mind because I'd long since decided I was an addict, not mentally ill.

I applied to the Peace Corps.

As escape plans go, applying to the Peace Corps is a slow burn. The application takes most of a year, followed by another indeterminate period before placement. This lag gave me plenty of opportunity to rationalize further, ultimately landing on the side of *fuck it.*

That first hit felt like peeling out of a wetsuit two sizes too small. I unfurled. Beyond the welcome stilling of my thoughts, I felt the reprieve of wholeness. The void inside me, that god-sized deficiency, was gone, swaddled in a blissfully gauzy tenderness I hadn't felt since Jeffrey died. *Ever?* Why had I not been availing myself of this comfort?

The next day I went to a bar for my first legal drink. I was twenty-seven.

When the Peace Corps at long last sent me to Tunisia, I found a new crew to drink with. Sweet relief, those chummy college years I'd missed. Until a screaming headache emerged and wouldn't go away. I grew restless. Couldn't sleep.

This manic phase eventually resulted in my medical evacuation from the Peace Corps, and another round of waking up without knowing where I was, only worse. I'd landed in Amsterdam. Dutch was in the air all around me, so English-adjacent, yet incomprehensible. For a time, I feared the others were speaking in tongues.

I befriended a woman I called The Countess.

The Countess wore loose diamond rings on her fingers, strapped up her chin as part of her nightly beauty routine, and usually wore at least two sweaters. She didn't have off-site privileges, but I did. I didn't have any money, but The Countess was loaded. When I went off the unit for group excursions, she gave me money I used to buy us beer. I'm not sure why this was permitted, but when I got back we'd sit around, smoking and drinking and talking. That's when The Countess told me how her husband started committing her to mental hospitals, just as her daughters were coming into their beauty.

"Those, darling, were the years of sleeping."

Eventually a nurse escorted me from Amsterdam back to the States, but not before The Countess stopped me to say goodbye. "Always wear a flower," she said as she pressed a fresh daisy into my hand. "Then people will see it's your special day and won't notice if you're sad."

A year and another institution later, I dragged my ass back into recovery to get off the drugs. Though I only meant the prescription ones. And here's where the story gets sticky.

After a couple of weeks sober, I returned to the mental hospital where I'd last been sequestered to ask about getting off the meds. My vision was blurred and I was sure my prescription was the wrong dose. But I was confused and quite thin. When I tried to show the intake nurse the pills I was on so she could help me wean, I found only loose blister packs of laxatives. They didn't let me leave. For weeks.

L.L. Kirchner

During this institutionalization, my relationship to my mental health shifted, thanks to my roommate, Dominica. Burned on more than half her body, she told me she'd set herself on fire. And when a fire did break out in the hospital's chapel during our stay, she claimed she'd been the cause.

I wanted to know everything. How had she done it? What pills were they giving her? What was her diagnosis?

Her only response was a watery-eyed glare and a warning. "Back. Off." In that moment, I knew without question that there were fissures in my brain no amount of meds or sobriety could eradicate—I was just like Dominica.

Even after I left the hospital, my vision stayed blurry. Unable to return to work, I had to move back in with my parents. My sister and I celebrated my thirtieth birthday at a chain restaurant where she had a coupon. Though my initial intention had been to stay sober only long enough to detox, eventually I reclaimed my sobriety.

By the time I landed in India, I hadn't availed myself of anything beyond therapy in years. And now here I was, telling myself I wasn't mentally ill. Was this from all the "positive vibes only" of yoga?

I'd been telling myself that divorce was not the same as death, but the heart doesn't make distinctions in grief. My god-sized void had taken on the force of gravity. I feared being crushed by the weight of it. Whether or not I tried this vipassana, I could end up having another nervous breakdown.

Fanning myself with my t-shirt, I made a vow. Having seen my grip on reality become tenuous and slip, I should know what to look for. Should I sense I was losing that grasp again, I'd leave.

Straightening in the lawn chair, I hovered the cursor over "no."

I knew goddamn well, one of the hallmarks of insanity is thinking you're sane and everyone else is bonkers. The end of my marriage had just come as a complete surprise. What did I know about how I was doing?

Jimi Hendrix never called manic depression a myth, either. His song called it a *mess*.

BLISSFUL THINKING

Bangalore 2007

You've got to be kidding me, I thought as the driver stopped in front of a concrete wall. Scrambling out of the car, I scanned the cement blocks for a sign, something, anything, to tell me what to do next. The surface was bare.

Was I even in the right place? Only I could get lost and be late to a meditation retreat.

But this place looked nothing like the lush, verdant settings I'd seen online, environments meant to help me find my bliss while I sat in silent contemplation. I was standing on a treeless scrap of cracked earth, staring at a blank wall as my driver sped off behind me in the dirt. There wasn't even a road leading here. Was I in the wrong place? Or worse, was this the right place? It wasn't like I could call someone. No one knew where I was, least of all me. "Hi, can you come get me? I'm somewhere outside Bangalore. Near a wall."

Suddenly a ways down, a gate opened. A heavyset Indian man puffed past me toward a car I'd failed to notice. Beyond the opening, a squat row of buildings formed a courtyard albeit around another square of parched dirt. The resulting haze of dust made the place appear neglected.

To the left of the enclosure sat an Indian woman in a high-collared, 1980s-era ruffled dress. She turned to look at me from behind a plastic folding table, the glare from her oversized, pink Sophia Loren-style frames camouflaging her face. Extending her right arm while pumping her fingers into her palm, she beckoned me in. I looked behind me, vaguely amazed at her confidence I should be there. Only it wasn't so amazing.

I was a forty-year-old, green-eyed, bottle blonde American in wide-legged kurta pants and a Superman t-shirt. We were well outside civilization, let alone any tourist destination. Once the driver had left behind the dirt roads, even the wooden shacks that sold lottery tickets, cigarettes, and bootleg hooch had disappeared.

This must be the place, I thought, not entirely relieved as I entered and took a seat. Without a word, the woman pushed forward a sheet of paper, a long list of rules.

I was used to the no "hello." That was pretty standard in India, a land that continually astonished me with its baffling mix of open-hearted kindness and brutal honesty. I was more surprised she didn't comment on my eye.

As part of my transformational fervor, I'd recently had Lasik, vision correction surgery I'd long wanted but feared. "You should absolutely do it," Debra, my host in

Bengaluru, had said. "The office is completely high tech. It's a myth that this country is third world—there are more millionaires in India than in the U.S. My driver can take you."

Lying in the cold antiseptic room—one eye covered, the other with the cornea flipped aside—I was sightless but still aware of people scurrying around. *This must be what it's like to die*, I thought, which was terrifying. So when the doctor went for my second eyeball, I flinched. The suction cup missed the mark, and I was left with an eye that turned Christmas décor—a bright red and green ball—as opposed to simply bloodshot. It took months to heal. Though hideous to behold, it didn't hurt. Plus, my vision was better than ever. I'd grown used to strangers, in that polite yet blunt way I'd encountered across India, pointing and demanding to know, "What is wrong with your eye?" It was a question I'd grown to love because, at least when it came to this aspect of what could be wrong with me, I had an answer.

Or maybe the woman had said nothing because the silence had begun?

I looked down at the paper.

No stealing, no sex, no killing. Check.

No talking. Precisely what I'd signed up for.

No reading. Damn, I'd been thinking this would be a good place to catch up.

Wait, what? *No writing*? How would I remember the insights I was expecting?

The kicker was what stopped me. *No food.*

Sophia Loren wanted the Pringles sleeve poking out of my bag. *Oh no, she won't.* Taking firm hold of the can,

I popped open the top and proceeded to stuff every last chip into my gullet as I marched across the courtyard.

One decree I hadn't missed in my cursory research was the center's twice-daily meal schedule. I figured they skipped a feeding because of the cost, which was free, or more specifically, donation based. The first donation I was ready to make was more food in the bank of me. As a hypoglycemic, I wouldn't make it on two meals a day. Especially not on top of mornings that began at the crack ass of dawn, presumably without the benefit of caffeine. Ten to twelve decaffeinated hours a day in cross-legged meditation would be rigor enough. Letting my blood sugar levels tank would make the ordeal unbearable.

As I stood chomping on my chips, I spied another car dropping someone off beyond the still-open gate. *If I moved fast enough, I could catch it.*

Then I caught myself, remembering my ex's words from the one in-person discussion we'd had since the divorce decree. The only reason he showed up was because I'd forced his hand by repatriating our dogs.

What had been arranged as a Stateside lovers' rendezvous turned into a perpendicular face-off. Our exchange—across the green-striped, prickly woolen couches that my mother had dragged from Pennsylvania to Michigan to Alabama and then back—was reduced to negotiations for our dogs, two fur babies he'd not only abandoned, but not once asked about since leaving Qatar. Yet I longed to jump to his sofa and burrow into his side.

I settled for asking, "Why do you want a divorce?"

"I don't feel like being married anymore," was all he'd say.

As I stood on the vipassana center's thirsty ground, licking salt from my fingers, I remembered his words, relating. I might not have been the one to quit my marriage, but I was adept at leaving. The circles I'd ridden around the Rust Belt as a kid had established a pattern—I grew itchy if I stayed in one place too long. To scratch at that agitation, I'd abandoned numerous lovers and jobs. I didn't want to be someone who quit when I didn't "feel like" doing something hard. This was why I'd signed up for a vipassana in the first place.

My deepest wish was that ten days of sitting in silence would reveal the hard truths about myself that years of self-inflicted toxic positivity had failed to erase. Otherwise I feared I'd never move on.

I strode back toward the front gate.

MEETING MY INNER BITCH

Bangalore, 2007

Returning to check-in, I tossed the empty Pringles can into the bin and handed my valuables over to Sophia Loren, whose nametag I now noticed read, "Sangeeta."

"You must sign here," Sangeeta simply said, pushing the paper back at me. In addition to the rules, she had the application I'd filled out online. She wanted my signature on both.

After a brief if laconic tour, during which I noted we had three private toilet stalls and running water, Sangeeta led me to the women's dorm just beyond the check-in. For the next ten days, my home would be this rectangle of concrete where twin beds lined the long walls. I shoved my bag under an empty cot; there wasn't even a bedside table. Not that ashrams were meant to be fancy, but this struck me as more barren than necessary.

No sooner had I finished that thought than I began scoping out the other women in the room. I wasn't sure if the *no-talking* rule had begun, only that no one did as we unpacked. We didn't even look at each other and smile, at least not after I remembered what I'd learned at the teacher training.

After passing a woman I'd never seen around the shala before, I said hello. Averting my gaze, the woman bowed her head, tapped her chest, and—after allowing for ample time to read the words she'd pinned there—turned away. I asked Jenny about it later. "She was wearing this weird, hand-printed nametag that read, 'In silence.' What was that all about?"

Tightening her ponytail in such a way I suspected I'd annoyed her, Jenny said, "When a person is in silence, you're supposed to stay out of their space. Not even eye contact. Definitely no talking."

Turning my attention away from my fellow vipassana meditators left me with nothing to do. Though I'd brought only one small tote and knew exactly what was in it, I could double check. Reaching under my bed, I yanked the canvas satchel out to survey its contents. T-shirts, sweats, and a hoodie for cool nights. Underwear. No socks. I could get away with one or two bucket laundries. Thanking the gods that Debra had let me keep the rest of my things at her place, I tunneled into a fresh diversion. *What would it be like to be financially supported by a partner?*

Gingerly fingering the pen, notepad, and graham crackers I'd also hidden inside, I peeked around to be sure no one was looking. Ferreting out my contraband, I slipped the stash into my pocket. Despite the illicit inventory, I was taking this endeavor seriously. Or as seriously as I felt I could because, also, I really did not want to lose my mind. Taking notes was supposed to help keep track of my sanity, but where would I do any writing?

In a flash I knew: The toilet.

Determined to capture these precious thoughts, I marched toward the only private space—the bathroom stall. I was still crouched inside writing when the bell rang. Time to start.

We streamed in silence toward the meditation hall, more of a tent really, a low structure with a tarp roof held up by wooden poles. The makeshift ceiling flapped in the breeze, a gentle *thwap, thwap*. Rows of meditation cushions were meticulously laid out. On the ground. As in, in the dirt.

A doughy Indian man in a saffron-colored robe called our names and pointed out our cushion assign-ments, men on the left, women on the right. To avoid the others' personal space, I studied the earthen floor on the way to my cushion in the second to last row. *What have I gotten myself into?*

At the front of the room, the robed man stood behind a podium atop a raised platform. Behind this dais was a plastic table with nothing on it. Unlike other Indian shrines I'd visited, there weren't any images of Buddha or other gods, flowers, or—and for this I was grateful—

incense. Just the dais, cushions, and a clock over the door behind us. Was the lack of visual and scented distraction a compliment to edicts against food and reading and writing, another layer of protection against external stimuli?

Once we were all seated, the robed man pulled a 1980s-era boombox out of the podium, set it down, pressed play, then took his seat at its foot. A disembodied voice, thick with India, poured forth from the speakers.

"Vipassana meditation was rediscovered more than twenty-five hundred years ago by the Buddha," the mysterious speaker began.

A tape recording?

"This non-sectarian technique," the speaker boomed on, "aims for the total eradication of mental impurities."

I managed to find a cut-rate version of a free service?

"Focusing on the connection between mind and body, you experience directly the physical sensations in the body, and the mind becomes balanced."

I wasn't sure if the guy up front would start talking when the tape stopped, but as the recording droned on I wondered, *When do we get to the silence part?*

Later I'd discover that the man behind the sound, S.N. Goenka, was a big deal. A successful businessman turned master meditator, he'd resuscitated this once-obscure style of meditation from monks in Nepal. By the time I understood that Goenka would be coaching us via tape deck for the duration while the robed man sat in silence, I'd stopped caring. His voice was compelling. I wanted what he sounded like, pure joy.

"Vipassana meditation will replace your suffering and

misery with love, compassion, and goodwill."

I wanted that more than anything. There was just one problem.

"Breathe in and out through your nose," Goenka said. "Focus all your attention on your upper lip, and feel the sensation. The sensation of your breath making contact with the upper lip."

Shaking my head, I shifted into the classic meditation position—spine straight, balanced on the sitting bones, belly soft, eyes closed. Was I even breathing?

"Constantly, you are aware of the breath. Incoming breath, outgoing breath."

I tried again, breathing slower. Still nothing. Was I having this issue because I started smoking when I was ten?

"Focus all your attention directly below the nostrils where you feel the breath."

My breath on my face? *Is he kidding?*

I exhaled more forcefully. Nothing.

Am I totally screwed?

Determined not to swivel my head—even *I* knew I wasn't supposed to move—I cracked my eyelids. But this view revealed only the backs of a few heads and the cross of our leader's legs. Aiming for subtle, I slid my chin slowly, only to behold my fellow meditators, rapt in still, placid bliss and seemingly unperturbed by these ridiculous instructions.

Liars.

In what felt like a stroke of genius, I curled my lip while pushing out an exhale. *There! I felt a stirring. Under my nose even!*

L.L. Kirchner

"Work with full effort, yet without any tension."

Relaxing my face, I licked my upper lip. It worked. So long as I kept my chops moist, I could feel my breath easily. I was totally making this work.

"Natural breath, normal breath. As it is. Just remain aware. Do nothing."

Before I could launch into another critique of the instructions, my neck seized. It felt like someone was stabbing me, inserting a knife to the hilt and twisting the blade.

"Focus all your attention under the nostrils, on this area of the upper lip."

What about my neck?

Jerking my head now, I found the clock. Thanks to the Lasik, I could actually read it.

Approximately three minutes had elapsed.

"Vipassana meditation is like a surgical procedure," Goenka said. "We are clearing away debris at the root level of the mind."

Yeah, a surgical procedure without anesthesia.

"We are constantly making choices," Goenka said. "Pleasant sensation, I like this. Unpleasant sensation, I don't like that. Craving, aversion. Craving, aversion. It becomes a never-ending cycle of suffering."

Whoa. His words described exactly what I'd been doing, deciding what I did and didn't like about the center, the rules, Sangeeta.

"Deep inside, one keeps reacting, and so one keeps suffering. Until we break the cycle, we will go on suffering."

Being in a constant state of dissatisfaction was how I

61

wrecked my marriage, I thought in the way I had then of turning everything into that story. *Do not cry. Do not cry. Do* not *cry!*

"Vipassana will teach you to stop reacting, stop suffering. You will find a never-ending source of joy."

How I yearned for a steadfast happiness that didn't depend on other people, places or things. But such a feat sounded more fantastical than finding Oz. Life had been one long exercise of attempting to acclimate in hostile environments based on what I could observe. This pattern had begun during my family's constant relocations, though as an adult I kept the churn roiling, casually switching jobs and continents. My strategy had been the same since childhood—investigate, imitate, correct and start over—keeping me emotionally occupied, always playing catch-up.

As I came to that realization, stake-like daggers dug into the underside of my thighs and buttocks. My ankle was on fire, but my feet were freezing. A searing pain wrapped around my hips. I looked longingly toward the door behind me, just under the clock.

I should leave now and get this farce over with.

But physical agony was not something I'd bargained for. The only out I'd given myself was in case of mental anguish.

Thinking over my escape—could I even get a driver out here this late at night?—I rested my cheek on my knee, affording some relief as well as a good look at the woman beside me. White like me, her posture was the very image of Zen. But how? She had to be at least one, if not two, decades older. Then again, she wore monk's robes and sported a shaved head. This probably wasn't her first round at a meditation retreat.

Deciding she was also sad, I imagined her freshly divorced, like me. Until I spotted her wedding band. Maybe she was a widow. Wasn't that a tradition in some cultures, shaving your head when your spouse dies? But she was Western. Or was she? Whatever she's upset about, she's obviously very serious. I nicknamed her, Humorless Shrew.

A cramp in my neck necessitated lifting my head and rolling it, which turned out to be the perfect move for sizing up the room. Behind me on the right sat the three Indian women I'd seen in the dorm, all in a row, impeccably turned out in their saris. Older even than the Humorless Shrew, I decided they were sisters-in-law with difficult husbands, all trying to make peace before their time was up. Maybe one spouse had died, and, seeing how much better it made her life, the other two had poisoned their partners. Obviously, all three were in cahoots. Could two women in the same family get away with that? After trying and rejecting several monikers, I went with The Cabal.

Hugging my knees, discretion be damned, I spotted a third Western woman, decked out in fisherman's pants, a yoga top, with a pair of chunky wooden pegs poking through her ears. *Straight from the I'm-traveling-in-India playbook*, I judged. Most damning, however, was her posture. Not only was she still as a stone, she sat in full yogic lotus, cross-legged with her ankles tucked into her hips. Was she kidding with that shit? My *face* hurt. Her I dubbed, Lotus Pose.

Not long before this vipassana, I'd been given a recording of Pema Chödrön, a Buddhist teacher. In it, Chödrön compared people beginning meditation practice to children with scabies, old enough to scratch the itch but not old enough to know that scratching makes scabies worse. Her point was that symptom relief didn't address the root of a problem. Chödrön's talk reminded me of what a mentor in sobriety had told me early on, "Drinking isn't your problem. You're not drinking anymore. Your problem is your thinking."

I'd agreed with my sponsor then, and would've done the same from my cushion in that meditation shed, even as the out-of-control and judgmental thoughts ran wild in my head. Trepidation about a potential nervous breakdown aside, I would've also said I was at this retreat to give my meditation practice a fine-tuning.

Since entering recovery some twenty years before landing at the vipassana, I *had* been meditating. My earliest sessions involved throwing down a Windham Hill record and visualizing myself aloft in outer space till I fell asleep, the only goal to de-stress. My practice hadn't evolved—except musically, I'd gravitated toward ambient "Buddha Bar" sounds—until I practiced Ashtanga yoga in Qatar and discovered that relaxation was not the aim of this particular meditation style. The goal was transformation through self-observation. This was the perfect whip with which to throttle myself.

No wonder I only ever found my Inner Bitch. I wasn't meditating properly.

From my uncomfortable perch in that ashram, barely tolerating the instructions, I convinced myself that I should look within even more microscopically. I had not a clue that vipassana practice was meant to help me pay less attention to the stories my brain loved to tell.

Suddenly I heard a change in the tape, specifically in Goenka's voice. At times I couldn't make out what he was saying, but this sounded straight up like a foreign language. Was he speaking Hindi? Sanskrit? Was that singing? Were we going to have to listen to a lot of this?

But no. The robed man stood, shut off the boombox, and rang a bell. The session was ending.

I checked the clock. More than an hour had passed.

While lost in thoughts of my fellow meditators, I'd been able to ignore the uselessly repetitive instructions to feel my breath. Maybe these ten days were the window of opportunity I needed to determine how I'd wrecked my marriage so *that* wouldn't happen again. Also, I needed to work out a career strategy that would sustain me for the rest of my life. Plus decide where to live, though the job might dictate that.

So much to unpack.

What is contemplation if not reflection?

To be fair, Goenka himself came across as a fan of introspection. "Develop your awareness of the present moment, so the past can be a guide to order actions in the future." That line was all the clarion call I needed to dive into my past with abandon. I missed his point about the present moment.

He also told lots of stories.

That first night, he'd relayed how anger had driven him to meditate. If I, too, could be rid of suffering, it was worth fighting to stay. Unless I was losing my mind, of course. Otherwise, failure was not an option, because I was out of alternatives. I knew if I didn't rid myself of this suffering, I was in trouble.

When Jeffrey had died, after taking a few days off to organize his memorial, I went right back to my old routines. I'd reversed recovery's maxim about relapse— "if you keep doing what you did, you'll get what you got"—into a dictum about sobriety. *If I keep doing what I did before to stay sober,* I'd figured, *I'll stay sober.*

But I was wrong, and this time I wanted to change before I relapsed. I might not survive it. Or worse, I might. Thus I lit upon the idea most diametrically opposed to the purpose of the sit: I would think my way through.

Yes! Me and my glorious THINKING!

All I had to do now that I'd decided to stay was walk to my cot. Only, I couldn't stand.

My legs were numb and I couldn't feel my feet. Rolling onto my right hip, I extended my left leg. In a quasi-down dog attempt, I pushed into my palms and tucked the toes of my left foot into the ground to hoist my right knee to the ground. Then I forced my right foot forward, and rose from there. Hot spikes seared into my feet as the ground took shape beneath me. I was proud I managed not to gasp. Not that anyone would've heard. I was the only one left in the room.

Even The Cabal beat me out.

L.L. Kirchner

JACKHAMMERS AND CHAIN SAWS

Bangalore, 2007

Sweat trickled down my neck and I fought the urge to wipe it away. Plastic sheeting overhead rustled in the breeze. A distinctly Pac Man-esque *waka waka waka* emanated from the poles, clearly termites gnawing their way through the wood. I wondered if the roof would collapse before I did.

Or I was hearing things.

"Staaart…" Goenka's voice rumbled. "Aagaaaainnn."

All our boombox sessions began with the words, "start again," but at an increasingly slower pace. By day four those syllables escaped at a crawl.

Suspicious he was trying to fill the time too, I wanted nothing more than to rip that tape player out of the wall and smash it over someone's head. Pain scorched my lower body—how was anyone feeling their breath?

"Agitation in the body," Goenka said, "is a manifest-tation of agitation in the mind." Now he was taunting me? I cranked my way up to standing and tottered toward the head, eager to commit these precious insights to paper.

Once I'd written all I could remember, I scratched the word PLUM into my notebook, an acronym I'd learned from my first mentor in sobriety, Ruth.

We were seated at a booth in a Columbus diner when I'd started in on my grades. "Shouldn't they be getting better now that I'm sober?" I asked.

Flipping her paper placemat, Ruth hunched over our table to pen the initials slowly and upside down to be sure I could read them.

"Plum," she said, tapping each letter for emphasis. "Poor. Little. Ugly. Me."

Ruth loved a slogan, especially if she could pair it with a mnemonic. She'd taught me all the basics, like: "Your best thinking got you here." And, "Easy does it but do it." Also the old chestnut, "Feelings aren't facts." Such doctrines had helped me get sober, turning victimhood into agency, but—I was beginning to suspect—to my detriment.

Now she circled the word several times. "Looks like a turd, right?" She looked up at me with her trademark half grin, her soft brown eyes glowing behind her eyeglasses. "But you are not the piece of shit at the center of the universe, no matter what your grades are."

In her sixties at the time, Ruth was a tiny human. She made up for her small stature with a stunning array of brightly colored turbans, not what I'd have expected from a retired Ohio schoolteacher. But then, I was nineteen and newly sober and had no idea what to expect. I'd been told I needed a sponsor, a woman who'd been in recovery at least a year and could teach me the essentials.

Maybe it was my pink hair and punk rock t-shirts—also nonstandard gear for Columbus, Ohio—but I was thrilled to have found anyone willing to work with me. Four or five other women had turned me down.

"Your mind is like a bad neighborhood," Ruth said, taking a drag off her cigarette. "Don't wander in there alone."

Suggesting I should run my plans and concerns by her made sense. I was practically feral. Ruth had already advised me on everything from classes to men to remembering to brush my teeth. If I wanted to be in control of my destiny, I needed to take responsibility for my actions and my experiences. Everything.

To someone who'd felt battered by circumstances outside my reach, the promise was irresistible. If everything was my fault, then I could fix anything. For whatever I hadn't yet fixed, there was another catchphrase. "Fake it till you make it!" Or, "If it ain't broke, don't fix it." Or the charming, "Keep it simple, stupid."

When Goenka said, "Once you are aware of how the mind is working, it becomes natural to be peaceful and happy," I heard the same accountability tenets I'd learned in recovery.

I even rationalized my discomfort.

In yet another misapplication of a self-improvement axiom—"there is no growth without pain," I reasoned that my misery was a sign. *Of course I'm miserable. I'm growing!* I was nothing if not determined. *And I will crack this breathing thing.*

Though I'd never tried to "feel the sensation of my nose hairs moving," even Jenny had commented on my breath before I'd ever heard of a vipassana.

"You need to let go of your anger," she'd whispered in my ear during an adjustment in class.

I must've given her an odd look; she explained right away.

"It's showing in your breathing while you practice. You won't be able to control your breath till you lose the anger."

No doubt I was angry. The papers for the divorce I'd been forced to organize had barely arrived before I left Qatar. What could I have been mad about when I started smoking?

From my perch in the stall, I wrote into my memories. I'd never attributed my substance abuses to anything I learned at home. My mom smoked, but my parents weren't drinkers—certainly they didn't use drugs—so, what emerged on the page surprised me.

Long before my first cigarette, I'd wanted desperately to be older. Nestling my feet into my mother's shoes, I'd rest my feet on the coffee table and watch *Speed Racer* over the toe boxes. Even before that, I could remember watching old black and whites with mom when I skipped school.

I wrote, "Did I start smoking and drinking because I wanted to be like the women in those films? They let the world know they were in charge, not empty shells upon which others imposed their will."

Fidgeting in the stall, I rolled my shoulders, picturing myself in my father's green pleather Lazy Boy. My mother was vacuuming. Each time she turned her back, I'd reach for her smoldering butt, lock my lips around the filtered end, and exhale. But I never matched her great puffy gales.

Bangor Elementary taught me my mistake. There must've been twenty of us out behind the Bay City, Michigan school, huffing on a single butt that afternoon. Ever on my quest for popularity, I was excited to be included. They could've been passing napalm, and I'd have stood there itching for it.

"Inhale, you dipstick!" shouted Randy, the boy beside me. Soon, he would gift me a tub of frosty blue Aziza eyeshadow, and we'd be going steady.

That circle never formed again, but I kept smoking. *Why did I keep smoking?*

Gnawing on the end of my pen, I questioned where I was going with this memory. As an adult I'd come to despair my lack of constancy, but as a kid I loved moving.

Or did I?

I'd been a bedwetter and a biter. One of my earliest memories is of wailing in bed for hours because my parents forgot "huggy-kissy time." Their attempt to follow Dr. Spock's advice for parents—the let them cry-it-out method—was a disaster, according to my mother. My lamentations didn't stop until my parents relented.

I wrote, "I was born with an insatiable neediness."

My drinking began in a similar fashion. Again I could

see myself—younger even, at our split-level in Greensburg, when I would've been a toddler—scrounging sips
out of glasses when my parents were in bed after a party.
But I didn't get drunk till I was ten, the same year I
learned to smoke. Only this time I made all the
arrangements.

During my mom's afternoon *Another World* nap, I
stole into the waist-high kitchen counter that served as
their liquor cabinet. Pouring from every open bottle, I
filled an old plastic Slushie cup. Stash procured, I pedaled
my bike over to an unfinished subdevelopment, one hand
on the handlebars, the other on my precious goblet.

My best friend Becky was already there, waiting. The
plan had gone off smoothly, until we finished the drink
and Becky started crying. Me, on the other hand? For the
first time in memory, my all-consuming need for
validation vanished. From there on, I would chase that
peace whenever possible. Though sometimes Becky and I
would smoke together, drinking became a solo activity.
Never for a moment did I think this behavior was normal.

*Was using how I'd coped with feeling like I didn't
matter?*

Sliding my pen and notebook into my pocket, I shook
my head, dismissing my feelings. Even if feelings of
insignificance were the source of my anger, there was no
changing the past. *I really should get back to that shed.*

With the languid step of a tortoise, I returned to our
meditation hut.

"Feel the breath," Goenka was still saying when I

returned. "Feel the sensation of the nose hairs moving."

Still?

I'd only just returned and already I wanted to run screaming from the room.

Am I getting worse?

We weren't even halfway through the fourth day, but maybe now was the time to go because—

"Let your attention wander."

Wait. WHAT. After three days of nothing but nose, was Goenka telling us to free flow? Gawking openly for others' reactions, I found not one sign. Not even a raised eyebrow.

"Now that we have developed observation of respiration," I heard and my excitement wobbled. *Have we?*

"Move your awareness, head to feet, head to feet. Do not move so quickly that in one breath, you move from head to feet or go so slowly it takes hours. Work two or three inches at a time."

Okay, it wasn't free flowing, but still. I couldn't leave now. I had to give this new thing a try.

"Keep your attention moving, in order."

Slight as this change was, I was buoyed by the new direction. My frustration level became far less acute, and the agonies more manageable.

"You must learn to be aware at the experiential level. This is not intellectualizing. You are really experiencing."

At last, I was learning the art of vipassana. I felt giddy. Maybe I could do this.

Seconds into my joy, a cacophony erupted outside our hut in the unmistakable grind of a chainsaw. Followed by a jackhammer.

What. The. Fuck.

Now I looked around the room with accusation. Nothing. I hated everyone in the room.

What were they doing out there? Building the real meditation hall? How could the organizers have failed to mention the building site? Or maybe that explained the scant attendance, everyone else had known. No wonder I'd found a spot here. *Screw this. I'm leaving.*

Hoisting myself up, I waddled back out the door as if traversing a bed of nails. When I finally made it to the courtyard, the forthcoming construction was plain as day—it was a real meditation hall. *I was right!*

That sentence slapped me to my senses.

Another mentor in sobriety—Elaine, whom I'd started working with after my relapse—had shown me the folly of my need to be right. Long before we'd left for Qatar I'd gone to her, upset my then-husband had left me in charge of managing an unresponsive contractor.

She tilted her head, taking a moment before answering. "Well, honey, you may be right about that. But there's nothing you can do about it now. Would you rather be right or happy?"

Often as I still return to this advice, the push to be happy instead of aware is not the solid guidance I once thought. But there at the ashram, the words fit. No point talking myself into a rampage over something I couldn't change.

Maybe I could handle the noise, consider the racket a welcome distraction. Looking around the courtyard anew, the surroundings transformed. The dust, the tarp roof, the scorched earth—these weren't signs of neglect but consequences of the development. I'd been neglecting information that had been obvious all along.

"Don't leave before the miracle happens," I said to myself, parroting another tenet I'd learned in recovery. Instead of heading for the dorm to collect my bag, I hobbled toward the toilet to capture my thoughts.

Later that night while brushing my teeth, I surveyed the courtyard, alternately inspecting and spitting. The women's bathroom was perpendicular to the men's dorms. They must've had their own bathroom too, but I couldn't see it from where I stood at the long sink on the exterior wall. Just as I turned to rinse, I spied Lotus Pose sneaking behind the men's dorms. With a man!

Rage, my full-time lover, spiked within me.

They're probably going to talk and have sex right now. Loser! That is totally against the rules.

Shoving my toothbrush and toothpaste into my pocket, I broke the last of my snack crackers, causing me to, once again, spot my hypocrisy. Not that I didn't argue my case.

We might both have been breaking the rules, but I had that hypoglycemia diagnosis. All Lotus Pose had was a doomed, co-dependent relationship.

Stop.

Even I couldn't cosign that last condemnation. This was why I was here, after all. I didn't want my failed marriage to dictate my future and slip mindlessly into hating men, couples, or love. I wanted to live in a world where there was enough for everyone. To know that one person's gain was not my loss. My Inner Bitch reared its head.

I can't leave now. I've GOT to outlast Lotus Pose.

START AGAIN

Bangalore, 2007

The morning air held a chill that would disappear by breakfast, replaced by an oppressive humidity, reminding me monsoon season was coming and with it, the end of my stay in India. Yet as the first sit passed in absolute silence, the "what next" quandary was replaced by the giddy excitement permeating the room. Today was our last day.

When the session ended and the tape player was shut off for the last time, the robed man announced that we were free to speak. Without missing a beat, the woman who'd sat beside me throughout the course, the one I'd dubbed the Humorless Shrew, leaned over and said, "I guess we needed extreme meditation."

For a moment I was perplexed, until the blast of a rotary hammer pierced the air. A joke. The Humorless Shrew was making a joke. About the noise.

"And I'm definitely not telling my husband about the whole sankhara thing," she said, her eyes crinkling as she rocked back in her seat. She was definitely American. "If we can pick up other people's karma just by brushing against them, imagine what sex would do."

Maybe Canadian?

"I'll never get him to come to one of these."

I snorted, recalling another talk by Pema Chödrön, the Buddhist monk. In it, she talked about the film *A Beautiful Mind*, and how the Pulitzer Prize-winning mathematician John Nash saw people who weren't there. She deadpanned, "How is that any different from what I'm experiencing?" As the Humorless Shrew disproved her nickname, it struck me that the world I pieced together was as made up as the one in John Nash's head.

On hearing my thoughts, notes from Pink Floyd's *Dark Side of the Moon* started up in my head. Was I starting to sound like a psychedelic rock album?

A sense of relief washed over me. My personality hadn't disappeared as I'd first worried, thinking meditation might make me so mellow I'd bore myself.

"Your ego will fight this practice with all kinds of lies," the philosophy teacher from our yoga course had said. "But you'll still be you. You won't suddenly prefer tea to coffee. You'll simply be less convinced that your preferences are correct."

I felt lighter, even as I clumsily maneuvered my way up and out of the shed. No one cared if I was the last one out but me. Whatever stories they were telling about me were only as real as the stories I'd been telling about them.

I lit up when the person who'd joined the session several days in—a woman with long dark hair and epicanthic folds around her eyes, a person whom I hadn't nicknamed but whose calm I'd noticed—touched my arm. "I think you were the most-improved meditator."

Lotus Pose nodded her agreement vigorously, and pride filled my heart even as the conversation shifted to plans. Or theirs did anyway. I still had none.

"Anyone going back to Bangalore?" I asked.

No one was, but rather than assume the real truth was that no one wanted to ride with me, I simply accepted the information. Welcome new behavior. Maybe this vipassana had been the fix I'd longed for.

Shortly afterward and still in this happy state, I was reunited with my phone. Because my mobile was barely a prototype and hadn't been used in ten days, it held sufficient charge to fire up. Among the emails was a letter from a friend describing a sublet in New York City's West Village. For $1,000 a month, she was offering a space in her apartment with a garden view, an elevator, and a dishwasher. Did I know anyone who might be interested?

"Yes," I wrote back immediately, punching furiously to turn the numbered keypad into words. "Me. More soon."

"I've fantasized about moving to New York forever," I told Debra over toast and jam. We were seated in the breakfast nook of her sumptuous Bengaluru apartment. Outside, the singsong of a fruit vendor floated toward us.

"Mango! Ba Na Na! Jackfruit!"

Debra nodded. "I can see you living there."

"Really?" I was flattered. "My mom always pounded into my head that the city was too dangerous and too expensive."

"It is expensive. What will you do for money?"

"Other than rent, between the public transit and free activities, New York is one of the least expensive big cities to live in."

Debra cocked her head. I wasn't sure I believed me, either. After six months of questing in India, I still had some savings but that wouldn't last. So long as there were no repair issues, the Pittsburgh rental would cover rent.

"I'm looking at it like going to grad school, but instead of giving money to a university, I'll spend it on rent and writing classes."

Before Debra could respond, her housekeeper arrived. Time for their morning ritual. Together they moved through the rooms, lighting incense and praying, paying particular attention to photos and small bronze statues stationed around the house.

Charmed as Debra's life was, I was too excited about my long-held dream coming true to compare. My search for redemption had obviously worked. I was ready to leave India. And pretty sure I was cured.

HOLY SHIT, I'M A WHAT?

New York City, 2007

Not long after returning from India, I found myself standing in line at New York City's Union Square Whole Foods, agog. This wasn't my first trip to the store, but between living outside the U.S. for three years, and inside New York City for the first time, I regularly marveled at the quotidian, and this checkout was a wonder.

The colorful lanes were divided by stanchions, while the overhead screens lit up, keeping the lines moving according to vocal prompts. The efficiency blew my mind.

"Blue is now open."

The swirl of humanity, however, took me back to the train station in Mapusa. When I went to the vipassana, I'd traveled by train. Not for the cost or sake of convenience—though the train was only about $5 compared to the plane's $45 ticket, the flight took only one hour as opposed to the ride's twelve—but because I wanted to experience this form of travel. What I hadn't bargained for was the difficulty level.

Buying the ticket was an exercise in stamina. At the depot, a clump of humans pushed toward ticket windows in no discernible order. If there was any directional signage, I couldn't see it from within the press of bodies. Not that I'd have been able to read them, everything was in Hindi. That made an impression. Owing to the many dialects in India, even in the less touristy spots English tended to be the lingua franca. Not here.

Once I'd squeezed my way to the counter, I was told to go to a different building, get a token, and come back. When I retrieved the plastic chit, however, the thing wasn't numbered and offered no additional organization. *WHY?*

"Yellow is now open."

Inching through Whole Foods, I shook my head at the memory and heard Goenka's voice. "The mind spends most of the time lost in fantasies and illusions, reliving pleasant or unpleasant experiences and anticipating the future with eagerness or fear." I could see my mind exaggerating this wait; I was doing so great.

"Green is now open."

I took two steps, only to be confronted by a couple—a man and a woman, maybe in their twenties, he, slender, she, all curves—full-on making out.

"Blue is now open."

Feelings of envy, loneliness, and homesickness for my life in Asia overtook me. In both India and Qatar, public displays of affection were non-existent. The former by tradition, the latter by law. In both, only men held hands in public, though not as couples. Or they weren't supposed to be anyway.

In Qatar, I'd hated the restrictions. In India, I'd forgotten about them. Now I wondered, did that physical distance enable my ex and me to drift? Rage bubbled. On top of feeling sad, I was mad at myself, Goenka's words completely forgotten.

"Red is now open."

I looked up. Not my turn yet.

Lisa, I reminded myself. *You're in New York Fucking City. Teaching yoga.*

Alongside the regular daze of culture shock, I was amazed that this had come to pass. I'd continued to practice without ever expecting I'd teach, and since the closest affordable classes were held at a gym, that was where I did yoga. One day I showed up, but the teacher didn't. The manager—whom I'd met because gyms were my family's business and maybe I'm chatty—asked if I'd teach the class. Without hesitation, I agreed. The money wasn't great, but it was enough that, with the income from my duplex, I was able to treat myself to practice at a proper studio. There I met more people in the yoga community and got more work. I'd just taught a class at Union Square's EastWest Yoga.

"Yellow is now open." My turn.

Moving to the register, I couldn't help but see the young couple again, still intertwined and now looking at a candle on the impulse-buy rack. The woman swiped a thumb across the back of her partner's neck, a heartbreaking gesture of familiarity. I had to bite my lip to refrain from crying as I checked out. Fortunately, speaking was not required.

Was I irreparably damaged?

Out front, I strapped my groceries to my rack and hopped on my bike to pedal home. I loved tearing through Manhattan on two wheels; cutting through the streets and traffic was the ultimate freedom. For brief moments I felt in charge of, if not my destiny, at least my destination.

As I often did, I played a dharma talk from meditation teacher Tara Brach to soothe myself, but her lesson only pummeled my heart further. Brach quoted Martha Graham about the ways our conditioning prevents us from engaging with the world. "There is only one of you in all of time, and this expression is unique. And if you block it, it will never exist through any other medium. And it will be lost."

My eyes stung. What was between me and being whole-hearted? No matter how many times I'd asked some version of that question, I couldn't answer. I'd heard far more devastating stories of heartbreak from others who'd gotten on with their lives. Even their romantic lives. Why was I still stuck?

I pedaled harder but could not hold back the tears.

Manhattan had kept me busy. Besides teaching, I was writing, taking classes, and going out most nights, whether it was to hear a famous author read, watch an uncensored film in the park, or go to a concert in short pants.

I'd arrived with a suitcase and since found my own

affordable studio apartment in Alphabet City. As proxies went, New York City was one of the most satisfying drugs I'd ever had. And like actual drugs, she'd left me completely uninterested in finding another lover. So much so, I'd begun to worry. *Have I hit the post-menopausal stage I'd dreaded where I'm done with sex forever?*

Seeing that couple at Whole Foods changed everything as my libido returned to the stage. Was not having a partner the block between me and being wholehearted?

"You don't get better at something you don't try," I could hear my mentor Elaine saying. Though she'd been referring to prayer, I was happy to twist this logic too.

Back home, as I struggled up the stairs with my grocery bags—*how did anyone manage with dog food?*—stopping to listen in the hallway for a stirring in my neighbor's apartment. At the sound of glasses knocking together, I slammed my groceries into the cupboard and bounded across the hall.

"I'll make us some tea," Sophia said by way of hello. At least a decade my junior, she had her life way more together than I did mine. At least she had a steady boyfriend, my primary criteria for selecting a worthy guide in this fresh endeavor.

"When's your next class?" I asked, but guessed it wasn't anytime soon. It was almost noon and she was still in her jammies holding an armload of dirty dishes.

"Come in, I need the break," she smiled, pushing open the door with her foot and heading into her galley kitchen. "I've been grading papers all morning."

Our apartments were the same, a bathroom at one end,

kitchen across from the door, and a large open space beyond. After dropping her dishes into the sink, Sophia made tea. Over a steaming mug on her crowded café table, I told her I was ready to try dating again.

"Just thinking about introducing someone new feels embarrassing. Like whoever I introduce my date to will be thinking, 'How long till you fuck this one up?'"

Sophia pushed aside some papers and joined me, dipping on her tea bag. "I don't think you have to worry about introducing anyone yet."

"What do I know? The whole of my dating life pre-dates Facebook and its demands for relationship status updates. And forget about caller ID. When I met my ex, I'd barely gotten used to how *69 made it impossible to remain anonymous if you called someone then tried to hang up," I said, searching Sophia's deep brown eyes for reassurance. "Online dating just seems so... *efficient.*"

"Maybe?" Sophia added. "I wouldn't know. I've never dated online."

"What? How is that possible..." I stopped myself before adding "for someone your age." Though my dating experiences now seemed charming, like cabbage rose wallpaper and chenille blankets, I was not entirely inexperienced with the concept of blind dates. "I used to write a dating column where I was essentially Match.com in the real world. People would send snail mail applications and I'd pair up couples."

"People mailed in applications?"

"Yes! So I know I need a decent picture. Will you take one?"

Sophia laughed. "Of course I'll take a shot for your

profile. Then you have to tell me all about it since I'll never do it."

Paying no heed to the implicit warning, I went at my new project with a vengeance. After all, thanks to my time in India I was not only healed, holy *shit*, I was a yoga teacher. Yoga teachers were supposed to be bastions of inner peace, wellness personified. Not lonely nutters cycling around the city in tears, afraid of going back on antidepressants because they, and therapy, were unaffordable.

Like a true soldier of toxic positivity, I would prove the former identity was me.

THE X-MEN

New York City, 2007

Being online sped up the dating process. I could meet a different man every night of the week, and for a while I did. But after pedaling twenty or thirty minutes to meet some guy from Jersey who felt the need to explain what a "trade show" was, even after I told him I was aware, or the attorney who talked nonstop, or a no-show, I was beginning to suspect I'd rather watch paint dry.

I checked in with Sophia.

"He asked if you wanted to go Dutch?" She was removing her mascara in her bathroom mirror while I leaned in the doorframe.

"You mean for the two coffees?" I asked.

"No," she said, her eyes going wide in the mirror. Aware I sounded like a bad feminist, I was more than a little pleased to see she was aghast.

"Yes," I said, matching her tone. "I told him, 'Well, I

guess I don't want to buy yours.'"

"But I thought he was a professor," she said, motioning toward her table. "You want some water?"

I nodded. "I guess that's the bad news for you. He's also still living at home with his parents."

Sophia almost spit out her drink.

"So I've decided I'm going to insist we speak on the phone before we meet."

Twisting her curly mane into a scrunchie and pulling it tight, Sophia looked me dead in the eye, very serious. "No one talks on the phone anymore."

Her words were like a dagger to my heart. "But how do people get from hello to good morning?"

"Beats me." She shrugged. "I met Tom in grad school."

Maybe I should go back to school.

Rationally, I knew that being in a relationship was not a mark of wellness any more than *not* being in a relationship meant I was unwell. But that was my head. My heart was another matter.

Despite how my marriage had turned out, I'd liked being married—the companionship, the shared jokes, the inner worldliness of it all. Then there was the sex. Fabulous as New York City was, as a boyfriend substitute, she left something to be desired. The random encounters I'd had were so far in the rearview, mothballs had gathered in my vagina.

I reimagined my dating strategy, limiting meet-and-greets to activities or events I would've done regardless of the company. That way the get-togethers didn't feel so much like Dates, and if someone failed to show it hardly mattered. And the city was awash in low-cost things to do—storytelling shows, museums, street festivals, etc. With grinding regularity, however, I was the one who picked the excursion. Until Xtopher.

According to his profile, Xtopher lived nearby, was gainfully employed, and wrote in complete sentences. But what was I supposed to call him? Xtopher? Xtoph? X? Or would that be Christ, like Xmas? After exchanging a few flirty messages back-and-forth, I was ready to meet.

`Call me`, I messaged, along with my phone number. Sorting out his name would be gentler that way, too.

But Xtopher texted.

Tempted as I was to ignore Xtopher, the text was an invitation. An invitation to a sold-out show for which I'd tried—and failed—to acquire tickets. Overlooking the texting part, I figured I'd ask what to call him in person.

When we locked eyes in the crowded bar later that night, my heart fluttered. Xtopher was exactly as tall and fit as his profile made him out to be. Better yet, his eyes sparkled when they landed on me.

"I'm Chris," he said, though he'd forever be X to me.

We spoke a bit during the show, but the band was loud. Our real connection emerged on the walk home.

X enjoyed the show.

I enjoyed the show.

X was a surfer.

I liked oceans.

X did yoga.

I did yoga!

When he asked if I'd like to go to a yoga class that weekend, it was clear this X was boyfriend material. When it was time to say goodbye, we found ourselves in a passionate embrace in front of his apartment, which just so happened to be closer to the venue than mine.

Feeling his chiseled body against mine, I felt self-conscious to be standing on a street corner. Unlike the suburbs where I'd lived before, cities had no private spaces. Though in the year I'd been in the city I'd seen everything happen on the streets of New York, I had no desire to join that throng.

"Let's go inside," one of us said.

Was it me? Him? Didn't matter. I didn't hesitate. I wasn't thinking we were about to have sex, but once we were inside his kitchen/bedroom, I was all in. I hadn't been laid in nearly a year, forget about how long it had been since I'd had it on a regular basis. Besides, I hated the gendered expectation that a man should have to wait. Women wanted sex, too. Plus, I was in the best shape of my life.

After a lifetime in an "average" body—neither thin nor thick—between the yoga and the biking, the goods had transformed. I wanted to show them off. I'd even worn a bikini unselfconsciously. Just at the beach, of course, but still, that was big for me.

In Xtopher's studio, I harbored no illusions we were about to "make love," but that was fine. Obviously we were heading toward that kind of intimacy.

The weekend came. And went. No phone call, no text, nothing.

I deactivated my profile and proceeded to weep in a

fetal position. I never heard from Xtopher again. For the first time since leaving Qatar, thoughts of steering into oncoming traffic returned, though the end of my marriage hadn't been the first time I'd thought of ending my life.

After Jeffrey drowned, I'd wanted life to be over. At twenty-four, I felt like it already was. In Qatar, the idea grew more distinct, visions of what would happen if I took my hands off the steering wheel. By India the thoughts had dwindled back to the more manageable level of wishing my life was over, until somewhere along the way they disappeared altogether. Now, however, those ideations returned. Only in New York City, I'd have had to propel myself into the oncoming cars.

Though desperately poor I called a psychiatrist, fearing and hoping he'd restart an antidepressant. *What if I couldn't afford the medication?*

I would have to worry about that later.

"The doctor can see you in eight weeks," the receptionist said. Very calm, like this was the standard.

"Eight weeks! What if I'm hanging from the rafters by then?"

"Shall I make the appointment?" Still calm as fuck.

Apoplectic, I took the time slot. What else could I do?

"The answer is always more spirituality."

Remembering my sponsor's words, I doubled up on my meditation. True to the style I'd concocted at the vipassana, I spent many hours on the floor, mired in thoughts of how I'd said and done the wrong things to Xtopher, my ex-husband, and even Jeffrey, who'd drowned almost twenty years prior. When I wanted to rake myself over the coals, no event was too distant.

Despite my misguided meditations, when the doctor's office called with an appointment reminder, I'd forgotten I'd even made one. I was fine, or at least fine enough I'd stopped wanting to end my life. Deciding that was adequate, I canceled, relieved I wouldn't have to worry whether I could afford the prescription.

Throughout all this—loath as I am to admit it—I kept at my hunt.

"What do you mean I should never have gone into Xtopher's apartment if I didn't plan to sleep with him? Who plans these things?"

"You wanted to date him, right?" Sophia and I were in my apartment, seated atop oversized canvas pillows I'd had made from colorful tent fabric back in Qatar. She was leaning against the wall, her dark hair a stark contrast to the brick surface I'd painted a bright fuchsia.

"I did see us dating," I said carefully. "But you know I don't buy into that self-helpy bullshit about women withholding sex. I slept with my ex-husband on our first date, and that didn't make him think I was damaged goods."

She paused, maybe hoping I'd spot the logical fallacy so she wouldn't have to point out how well that had served me. When I didn't, she artfully changed the subject.

"Don't you think that once you sleep with someone, it's easier to overlook the red flags? Especially if they're good in bed?"

I pulled my knees close and sunk my forehead into

them, genuinely confused. What red flags? The ex and I were different, of course, but how could anyone expect otherwise? I didn't want to marry my carbon copy any more than I wanted to have sex only with myself for the rest of my life.

"I see what you're saying," I lied, lifting my head. "But seriously, if there's a big disconnect on sex, do you really want to spend months getting emotionally attached and *then* find out the sex is bad?"

"Hey, I didn't say it took *months*. But I get your point." She shrugged. "I need more time to figure out if *I* want to sleep with them."

"I can pretty much tell right away."

We both laughed, but, luckily for me, Sophia probed past my tendency to deflect. "Didn't you say you weren't thinking so much about having sex till you got inside his place?"

"True. But I felt so weird making out in public. I'm used to the suburbs, where you have cars."

Sophia nodded. "And your bedroom isn't your living room. But here? After you go inside, it's over. There's no coming back from that. You need to *not* go in unless you plan to have sex."

"What has happened to me? I used to be so down for sportfucking. But now? Ugh. I feel like hell. And I only met the guy one time."

"You know that especially means it doesn't have anything to do with you, right?" Sophia asked, her dark brown eyes impenetrable.

"Does it? It feels more like there's a sign over my head that tells everyone exactly what's wrong with me," I said. "Except me. I can't see it."

"Well, I can't see it," she said.

"Oh, but I'm not trying to date you."

This time our laughter ended the conversation, except in my head.

One aspect of getting back on the market that I hadn't discussed with Sophia, or anyone, were my thoughts on children. Having my own biological offspring was out, but adoption was a possibility. I wanted to fall so deeply in love again that the urge would return.

If I clicked "yes" to wanting children, wouldn't it suggest I could have them? Did I have to lead with *that* conversation? "I'm fine with kids, but I can't have them. Menopause. But I swear I'm the age I say on my profile, the change came way early for me. Really!"

Yet "no" wasn't true, either. I had a negative reaction to someone who didn't have kids and expressly didn't want them. What if a relative was no longer able to care for their child? Or your best friend was in a tragic accident? Or you somehow got pregnant? Where was the box for that?

Ideally, I'd meet a man who already had a kid or kids. Preferably past the diaper stage. I narrowed my search to men my age and older.

A large number of men in their twenties emailed anyway. I rejected them out of hand. I couldn't imagine they'd look at me for anything other than sex, and I didn't want to experience that kind of rejection.

In truth, though I disbelieved the self-help dating

"rules," I lived with a prude-in-residence who kept whispering, *You should not have slept with that guy!*

My libido—no longer satisfied with its urban substitute—would need to be kept in check. Before jumping back online, I zipped across town to the Pleasure Chest, the West Village's erstwhile mecca of sex toys. They had every kind of device imaginable, at every price point. Though barely scraping by, I splurged. If I was going to put it in my vagina, I had to really like it, a standard more easily purchased than discovered in the wild. But I refused to espouse cynicism. I yearned for what the ancient Persian poet Rumi once wrote of: "This is love: to fly toward a secret sky, to cause a hundred veils to fall each moment. First to let go of life. Finally, to take a step without feet."

To find my way, I'd need another guide. Someone who thought outside the rules of the patriarchy. That's where Willy came in.

WILLY, NYC

New York City, 2007

New York City crawled with 12-Step meetings. I found a nooner I loved not far from my apartment, just past Tompkins Square Park. The time slot was a comfort. Noon meetings had played a huge role while I worked my way through college in my earliest bout of sobriety. As part of a twelve-hour rotation between work and classes, I hit meetings at noon and midnight every day for a year.

The midnight time slot proved unsustainable—even as a drunk I was barely a night person—but the noon meetings remained part of my repertoire right up to the end. Though it's "common knowledge" that going to meetings is the best way to avoid relapse, I managed to pick up while still actively attending meetings.

On this particular fall morning, the light had an amber quality. By the time I'd locked my bike outside the church where the noon meeting was held, the day had warmed considerably and I'd worked up a sweat. The night before I'd tossed and turned, reviewing where I'd gone wrong on my latest date. Mercifully, my seven a.m. yoga class had been packed. Teaching reassured me, in spurts anyway, that I was making a contribution to the world. That I was appreciated. As I climbed the steps that led into the meeting room, however, I felt the ineffable anxiety that I needed shielding, something outside myself to protect me from the world's harshness.

The person at the center of a couple dozen metal folding chairs asked for topics. I didn't bring up my sleepless night or the feeling I needed safeguarding. I never brought up any issues at all. I've been in and around recovery for more than twenty years. My contribution should be to help other people in the room, many of whom were counting days. Being of service was all the help I needed.

Deluded as that thought was, I nonetheless held fast to knowing there was no such thing as safely and forever sober. For someone with my form of the disorder, recovery is as much a practice as meditation is. Not that I feared relapse was imminent. The drug I feared most—surely a gateway—was my ex-husband. He lived far away, but I wasn't sure I wasn't actively searching for his double.

I didn't talk about that either.

"I'd like to talk about anonymity," said a young woman whose piercings and neck tattoos suggested she was not here on lunch from a corporate job. "I'm feeling really triggered by this essay my sister sent me? It's by some writer who supposedly went to rehab but is not sober? I thought we were supposed to be anonymous."

To my ears, the issues were separate. Why was someone else's recovery disclosure a trigger? If the writer wasn't sober, were they even breaking anonymity? Yet the room latched onto the topic of anonymity with a fury.

"It goes against everything in the book," said a handsome, mustachioed hairdresser who lived nearby and had cut my hair a few times. "Because what if I make a big announcement and then go back out? Then people can say, oh, recovery doesn't work."

His comment sliced. I'd said the same myself. Yet I was hard at work on a book that included my recovery. There was no honest way to portray my life otherwise. My fortieth birthday party in Qatar—an entire chapter in said book—was just such an example.

That year, my birthday occurred near the tail end of Ramadan, a month-long religious holiday observed by Muslims around the world. During this period, even the expats weren't able to buy alcohol, so I stockpiled a massive supply of booze. Omitting why it was so easy for me to hoard that liquor (and ensure a big turnout on a weeknight) made no sense.

Should only people *not* in recovery tell stories about addiction? Wasn't that how we'd ended up with so many romanticized *The-Artist-as-Lush* portraits?

More importantly, keeping my addiction a secret because of this prohibition had contributed to my relapse—no one outside recovery knew I shouldn't be imbibing, so when I did, no one raised an alarm.

"When you wake up to your own innate brilliance, none of this will matter," said a lanky man I'd seen at the meetings a few times, but not often. His words were like catnip. "You'll wear your sobriety like a loose cloak. You won't be so easily triggered. I'm sorry that you were. It took me a long time to take off the armor and curl up in a sweater—I've been sober almost twenty years—but it didn't happen because I forced it. The letting go just finally happened."

I had to talk to that guy.

Before leaving for Qatar, I'd begun to wish for a different sobriety mentor. This desire ramped up on my return to the States. Much as I loved Elaine, who'd been with me since my return from relapse, I needed the change.

A tall health fanatic with a ready laugh, Elaine was a nurse practitioner with enough master's degrees to make her a doctor several times over. The reason I'd asked if she'd work with me in the first place was because she'd relapsed many many times but gone on to accumulate more sobriety than I'd had before going back out. The time mattered to me.

Accumulated time conferred a shared perspective, I believed. Also, there was a degree of flexibility that could only come with sober experience. I'd never advise a newcomer attend a birthday party with drinks like the one I'd held for my fortieth in Qatar, when I had more than a decade clean and sober. In the beginning, though, that rigidity is necessary.

The same was true for my mental health. I hesitated to share the story of my many institutionalizations, the flip-flopping beliefs around my diagnoses, and the extraordinary number of people in recovery who clung to the belief that their addiction was not a form of mental illness, as worthy of treatment as heart disease. I feared having an inexperienced sponsor and being susceptible at the wrong time. With Elaine I had no such qualms.

"Honey, if you're being honest with your doctor and they prescribe something, *not* taking your medication is not sober behavior. That's you thinking you know best. Playing God. That kind of attitude gets you in trouble."

With her full support, I had, at various times, taken prescribed meds to get through depression, stopping when I started forgetting to take them. When it came to my marriage, though, she was less helpful. Once I'd complained to her about my then-husband failing to do some task and her reply took me aback.

"I don't know what to say about that. I always thought of men like lipstick. You should change them regularly." She laughed, a deep throaty sound, as soothing as it could be vexing.

Because everything was subject to inquiry via the lens of my divorce, I'd often wondered if I'd still be married had my sponsor had more insight into relationships. As if couples counseling was a sponsor's purview. With the eight-hour time difference, Elaine and I had hardly been in touch when I lived in Doha.

As my sober experiences continued accumulating, I had questions I didn't want to ask her. Like the slogan, "you'll feel better after a meeting." Patently untrue, and a statement I found not only dismissive but damaging. I was pretty sure if I'd shared that doubt with Elaine, she'd have advised me to talk about it at a meeting.

These thoughts rolled through my head as the meeting wore on and more recovery platitudes were invoked, like, "don't use no matter what." But I didn't share.

When the discussion ended, I bolted out before the closing prayer to wait at the bottom of the steps, wanting to be sure I didn't miss the guy wearing his sobriety like a comfy sweater.

As the people departing slowed to a trickle, I worried he'd eluded me anyway. Wasn't he still in the room when I left? Till at last those iconic square eyeglasses emerged, my quarry attached.

"Oh hey," I said, trying to act casual. Though I'd never worked with a man—doing so went against recovery "suggestions"—I wanted to ask if he'd be my sponsor. Besides, I'd already asked every woman I'd met with any clean time; they had prohibitively full schedules.

"I loved what you said about waking up to your own innate brilliance."

He smiled. "Are you interested in Buddhism?"

"I just got back from a ten-day vipassana retreat in India a few months ago," I said, trying to mute my enthusiasm. Even if he wouldn't sponsor me, maybe he'd be a spiritual guide. I thrust my hand out. "I'm Lisa."

"Willy," he said. "Why don't you come chant the Daimoku with me?"

I had no idea what that meant, but I was game. My online dating fails left me with the sneaking suspicion I might still need some work. This could be the next path being laid before me. The vehicle for healing that would show me whatever it was that had made my ex-husband run away.

Over lentils at a patchouli-infused café nearby, we talked.

"You sure you don't want a female sponsor? I *am* gay, but…"

"I've never *not* had a female sponsor, but I've already asked a few women. From what I can tell, all the women here with any time sober are busy."

Willy squinted. Dammit. Was he sensing already that I was deeply flawed?

"It's not like I'm a newcomer," I blurted, thirsty. "I don't need to learn, like, how to stay sober."

"Why do you even want a sponsor?" he asked.

Sitting up straight, I tucked my chin into my neck and slow-blinked a few times, recalling how, when I'd first gotten clean, I feared that literal men in white coats would come and cart me back into the psych ward if I didn't do all the things sobriety asked of me. I don't know who I thought was keeping tabs, but this belief lent urgency to following the 12-Step program. I hadn't thought about that peculiar mental twist in years; the recollection made me pause. Why *did* I want a sponsor?

"In the pamphlet, *Questions and Answers about Sponsorship*," Willy went on, "it says that once you've done your ninth step, you don't need one anymore. Haven't you done your ninth?"

"Oh no, I've definitely made amends," I said. *Even to*

my dick of a former spouse.

"Then you need to find other people to work with."

This was a sensitive spot. In all my years in recovery, I could count on one hand the number of women who'd asked me to work with them. "I'm guessing you don't have a sponsor."

"You'd be right," Willy nodded. "Though I did, for years. Mel. Till he died of this goddamn virus."

At the meeting, Willy had also mentioned being among the earliest cohort of New Yorkers diagnosed HIV positive. He'd stayed sober anyway. "What is it you want to work on?"

As I began to describe the end of my marriage, my eyes welled. Fearing he'd never sponsor me if he knew what a mess I was, I tried to lighten the mood. "This phase is more about emotional sobriety," I said, remembering I wanted to look into that. "I mean, since my divorce, I can't get a second date to save my life."

Willy didn't react.

"I don't see it as traditional sponsorship so much as recovery accountability partners," I said, my neediness on full display. "How does that sound?"

Willy sighed but agreed. "This isn't gonna be one of those one-way deals where it's all just you dumping your shit. Deal?"

Deal.

We agreed to meet at his place, a few streets away from my apartment, where he'd teach me the chant. The Daimoku was sung by Nichiren Buddhists as their primary practice, a prayer that affirmed nirvana was possible in this lifetime.

"I have to warn you," I said. "I'm a terrible singer."

Willy laughed. "So am I."

"But you're in a band."

"Yes, but I'm a recording artist. Technically a mixing engineer," he said. "I mix other people singing. Very different."

With Willy I never felt judged, so I was as honest with him as I'd ever been with anyone. And for a long while we were good together.

MY DINNER WITH KEITH

New York City, 2007

Mom was on speaker as I stood in front of my full-length mirror, assessing my outfit options. *Should I go with the olive dress or the red corduroy number?*

"That old tightwad McMunn is complaining about the Silver Sneakers fee going up," she said, referring to a member at the gym my parents owned.

Pawing through my drawer in search of my gray tights, I sighed. I didn't mention the date I was getting ready for. Mom would've disapproved.

"Don't you think you two are better off as friends?" I imagined her asking, implying I was about to fuck up a good business contact. Not that she'd ever say "fuck up," Mom didn't curse. Worse, she wouldn't have been wrong. Keith was a published author with a long list of national bylines—we'd met in the writing class he taught—but he was so hot. Balding with a hint of ginger beard, he had a runner's body, long-limbed and square chested. Did I mention he was a writer?

"We don't set that price," Mom was on a roll. "It's a *third* of the regular rate as it is."

I had nothing to say. She'd been making the same complaints about that health club for decades, but I'd run out of sartorial edits. And patience. "Mom, I gotta run. I'm going to be late... for class."

Fast as I could pedal without melting, I raced to the restaurant. I'd gone with the red dress and low heels, an outfit that allowed for exertion and didn't scream DATE. Because maybe it wasn't? When the course ended, I'd emailed the essay I'd finished in his class, and Keith had written back suggesting we talk over dinner. When I said yes he picked an Italian place with tablecloths. That made it a date.

Right?

Keith was already seated when I arrived, followed almost immediately by the waiter. She wanted our drink order.

"Water's fine," Keith said.

"Water's good for me too," I said, ready for that whiff of disappointment that crosses a server's face when you failed to pad the tab. But she was good, nonreactive.

"Just because I didn't order a drink. Have a glass of wine..." Keith trailed off, shrugging.

When the waiter was out of earshot, I leaned forward, noticing how tonight's sweater was a raglan gray that pulled the blue from his steel-colored eyes. "That's something else I think we have in common, actually."

He looked puzzled.

I smiled. "I don't drink either."

"Oh."

Failing to drop the conversational nonstarter, I went on. "Between your essays in *GQ* and the *Times,* I figured you went to meetings, like me."

"You read them both?"

"Everything I could find."

Keith sat up straighter. "Oh? What gave it away?"

I pointed out the signs, phrases he'd used like, "Easy does it but do it." How, in another piece, when someone asked if he wanted a drink, he'd replied, "Not today."

"Normal people don't talk like that," I said.

Looking around the room, he shrugged. "Hmph. Ok."

"I thought, well, my ex—"

"Your *ex*? Husband?"

I frowned. He knew I'd been married. Didn't he? All my essays—

Then I got it. He was needling me for talking about my ex. This *was* a date!

I lifted my hands as if he were pointing a gun. "Guilty! Sorry. But in all honesty, I was intrigued by the fact you don't drink. The ex was a huge drinker. I didn't realize how much I hated it until—"

The waitress was back. "Ready to order?"

"Yes," Keith said at the same time I said *no*. He looked at me, lifting a hand. Just shy of shushing.

"I come here all the time. It's between my gym and my apartment."

Turning his attention back to the waiter, Keith

proceeded to order. For both of us. I didn't know if that was sexy or overbearing, but I liked his selections so I went with sexy.

"What were you saying? You're in AA. Please tell me you have more than a year."

"I've been in the program almost twenty years."

That perked him up. "Good! I can't tell you how many women I've met, they pick up a chip, leave the meeting, and sign up for OKCupid."

Definitely a date.

"Well, I did relapse in there," I felt compelled to mention. "So I only have eleven years." Yes, I said only eleven years. From what I'd read, I guessed Keith had been sober twice that long. Surely, he would understand where I was coming from.

"But I don't think you ever *lose* time."

"People who relapse always say that." He grinned.

Fuck me. I had to right this ship.

"But have you done your fifth step? I don't care if someone has fifty years. I don't think you're really sober till you've done your fifth. Have you done yours?"

Keith's face went disconcertingly blank. "Yeah. I think."

"You *think*?"

"I'm joking. I mean, we don't have to share our inventories now, do we?"

"Of course not!" I nodded. Then went on with my confession. "But time does matter to me. I started drinking after I'd been sober a while. Then my sober boyfriend died, and I went back out."

Lacking any response, I kept divulging.

L.L. Kirchner

"It surprised me, but when I got divorced I felt just as shitty. If I didn't recommit to sobriety by going to India to study yoga and meditation"—though not quite what I'd set out to do—"I would've relapsed for sure. The heart doesn't distinguish between death and divorce when it's breaking, you know?"

"How long did you say you've been divorced?" Keith asked.

"We were divorced before I left Qatar. So, almost two years now? It felt like it took so long at the time, I thought..."

I managed to stop before saying aloud how I'd hoped his silence signaled reconsideration. Those five months between sending the papers and getting them back had ached with possibility.

"I'm not worried about relapsing now," I said. "Back then, I think my relapse was how I processed my boyfriend's death."

Ignoring Keith's disinterest, I proceeded to poke at the distant past.

"He drowned. My boyfriend."

"Oh. Was he sober? When he died?"

I sat back, crossing my arms. Much as I hated the question, I wanted a witness, someone to hear my story. Someone who'd been sober a long time. Someone who would understand.

"He had like ten years. Why do people always ask that?"

Without waiting for an answer, I plowed on. "When I finally did pick up, it was horrible. Everything bad that happened when I was drinking happened again, only

111

faster and harder."

I shrugged. "The only reason I got sober again was to get off the psych meds. They had me on Trazodone for depression, Risperdal, for my thinking, and Haldol for, well, a whole whack of diagnoses… I lost it after that. In barely a year I went to three mental hospitals. Or four? I was on so many meds, my vision blurred. I couldn't watch TV, forget about reading or writing. But I did get really good at blowing smoke rings."

"You smoke?"

Blowing past his curious conclusion, I agreed my story was bonkers. "I mean, who finds out they can't have kids, gets a divorce, quits their job and moves to India, and then quits smoking?"

The waiter appeared with our appetizers and, rather than respond to me, Keith asked for the check.

In a debrief with Willy the following day, I made light of the situation. "Of course I mentioned psych meds. Why stop at only seeming crazy when I can make sure he *knows* I am?"

Willy laughed. "He sounds like a dick."

We were walking to the noon meeting and I stopped in my tracks. *A dick?*

"You slept with him, didn't you?"

"I did. So?"

"Hey, I'm the last one to judge. Was it good?"

"Oh my god, it was GREAT."

"Well, there you go."

"Now I just wish I didn't care if he called. But I mean,

we could be so great together. We're both sober. We're both writers. And the sex was great."

"Maybe he will."

And he did. Intermittently.

On those occasions Keith texted to see if I was around, I answered the call. Far better to meet up with him, a known entity, than try to meet someone online. Unlike the efficient marvel I'd initially embraced, I'd begun to see how internet dating turned people into products and me into a consumer. In its ecosystem of *NEXT!*, we were all replaceable.

In between, I read his work anxiously, afraid but also hoping to find some version of me in his words. Women played a large role in his writing, but I never appeared.

One day after messaging back and forth a few times, instead of asking to meet up, Keith informed me he could no longer be in a relationship with me because he "kinda sorta" had a girlfriend.

I stared at my monitor in disbelief, then looked out the window at the grocery store across the street and saw a kiss of fire in the trees. A season universally beloved, I dreaded the fall. As a child because of the anxiety of starting at a new school with my birthday impending. No one ever goes to the new kid's party. My birthday made me cringe, the reminder I was getting older and still alone.

Determined to role-play the cool girl, I turned back to my computer.

```
We only kinda sorta have a relation-
ship. And it works for me the way it
is.
```

Keith didn't respond. *Was he relieved?*

I messaged Willy.

```
Do you think I'm ready to recite the
Gongyo with your group?
```

He wrote back immediately.

```
I've been waiting for you to ask.
```

NAM MYOHO RENGE KYO

New York City, 2007

Willy and I were walking to the apartment where his friends met to chant. I was thrilled he was taking me along, especially since I still stumbled through the ancient words.

The lotus sutra—the prayer recited in Gongyo—was essentially the extended play version of the four-word Daimoku, *"nam myoho renge kyo."* Though I still wasn't clear how either was going to help me achieve nirvana, I enjoyed the Daimoku. Sending an important email? *Nam myoho renge kyo.* Before teaching, *Nam myoho renge kyo.* Or just bored, *Nam myoho renge kyo.* But I wasn't such a fan of the longer rendition.

My sort-of sponsor interrupted my thoughts, with a sigh. "New York's getting beautiful again."

I looked around in the fading afternoon light. Fall rains had stripped the trees bare and garbage bags were piled high onto the sidewalks, ready for the next morning's pickup. Was taking me to this meeting making Willy sentimental? Fishing for a compliment I asked, "What do you mean?"

"Everybody looks good in a sweater." He smiled.

A knot of knit-clad young adults passed and I nodded, thinking how different the stories we told were. Willy didn't just find the good-looking people in an environment, he was one of them. Far more put together than me, his look paired G-Star Raw tennies with skinny jeans and slim-fit tops, topped by those black square-framed glasses. He groomed to perfection, too, keeping his kinky hair cropped close at all times and his face smooth and clean-shaven. I was quite sure he only tolerated my Indian tunics paired with whatever leggings I'd taught yoga in, though my "look" did the job of hiding how infrequently I cracked out my razor.

We were both freelancers—Willy did sound engineer-ing—but he never worried about money like I did. Willy attributed this calm to becoming a Buddhist, specifically chanting. But what intrigued me was his steady stream of male companions. I was in awe of his prowess.

"Chant, and you'll know," he'd replied when I first asked how repeating the lotus sutra could be transformational.

But the knowledge eluded me. Much as I wanted to embrace his faith, I found the act of repeatedly intoning the lotus sutra unpleasant. The best part was when the chanting stopped and I could feel the sound waves reverberating throughout my body. Physically making the sound, however, aggravated my throat. My voice needed to be in good working order to teach yoga. A no-show was a no-pay, regardless of why. Plus, my history with Catholicism had rendered me permanently suspicious of religions.

"Buddhism isn't a religion," Willy had once said. "It's a philosophy. A way of looking at life."

With all the rituals, myths, and sacred objects I couldn't see the difference, but I didn't bring up my opinion again.

We arrived at the building where Willy's group met, an ordinary Alphabet City walkup.

Sandalwood incense wafted down the steps as we climbed toward the apartment. We joined about a half dozen people on the floor, encircling a shrine that featured a framed copy of the chant (sadly in Japanese so, useless as a crib sheet), flowers, bowls of water, photographs, and an orange. The altar took up a lot of room and made me curious as to the size of the place, but now wasn't the time to ask for a tour.

Willy motioned for me to sit beside him. We went around the room with each person introducing themself, and—as if we were at a recovery meeting—the room burst out in applause.

Do not say, 'I'm Lisa, and I'm an alcoholic,' I warned myself.

Next, we chanted as a group. For a long time. During this musical interlude, to my surprise, attendees moved about. At one point I went to the bathroom to give my throat a break, feeling a lot like I was escaping a vipassana sit.

When the singing ended, I did feel renewed. Chanting

as a group had more power than my solo at-home efforts, even those where I queued up Tina Turner on YouTube and sang along with her. And I loved the promise—through chanting you would glow with love, drawing bounty into your life. You became radiant. As I sat, post-chant, enjoying the full body reverberation, I believed the assurances. Then the host started the discussion.

"When we chant nam-myoho-renge-kyo, we eliminate evil karma, so we can manifest good fortune and benefit."

"Nam-myoho-renge-kyo," the group replied. We might as well have been saying, "Glory to you, oh Lord." The words kind of mean the same thing.

Our moderator then went on to speak of his ambitions at work, ambitions he hoped would fuel renovations for the apartment he and his wife shared, and for the children they planned to have. It was all sounding more than a tad transactional.

"Nam-myoho-renge-kyo."

Going around the circle, each person shared some aspect of the sutra they were feeling, then expressed a desire for the group to affirm. This made me wildly uncomfortable. Willy hadn't warned me about this part. Could I skip my turn?

Luckily, Willy was seated to my right and went before me.

"Every person has the capacity to become enlightened," Willy said. "I want my music to have that impact on other people. *Lots* of other people."

"Nam-myoho-renge-kyo."

My turn.

What I wanted was a boyfriend, but I'd die before

admitting that. I wanted money, too. The raging success of a bestseller. Movie rights. A guest appearance on *Saturday Night Live*. Not that I'd admit to my far-fetched desires. But I could copy Willy. "I want my book to help people see the universal nature of suffering."

As the next person spoke, I mulled over those words. My book was about divorcing while feminist in a highly patriarchal culture, but that was just the plot. I did want the stories of how I'd internalized misogyny and racism to show others how they might have too. Not merely to understand, but to change. Although happy I didn't have to fabricate, I wasn't relieved after my share. I'd asked for something that couldn't be conjured.

"It seems weird," I said to Willy as we walked home, emboldened by the dark. "We're chanting to get things."

"Chanting to get things? Hmm."

"Like that guy who wanted a raise at work. Or that woman who wanted to go on a trip..." I trailed off. Wasn't it obvious?

"You've said before you want a spirituality that works in all areas of your life, right?"

I nodded. "I do want that."

"Why shouldn't money be a spiritual area of your life?"

I didn't want to disagree; I wasn't even sure I did. But the thought of spending my time in communion with the divine wishing for a boyfriend felt off.

"Wouldn't a spiritual approach to money be to accept what you have?"

Willy stopped walking and looked at me. "Why would you want to ask for that?"

Was he upset? "But isn't that the grasping opposite of what we learn in recovery? The whole, 'Be careful what you pray for. You just might get it.'" I laughed, attempting to discharge the awkward moment.

Willy shrugged and started walking again. "Maybe Nichiren isn't for you."

That hurt. Like he was taking away something before I'd made up my mind. Plus, I didn't want to be broke. Or perpetually single. We reached the end of the block and it was time to go our separate ways.

I was afraid to ask, but I had to. "I hope we can still work together anyway?"

Willy pulled me in for a hug. "See you at the nooner tomorrow."

Such acceptance was unlike anything I'd ever experienced, sweet relief. But I let the moment escape and wondered instead, Was there anything left to try?

What if I went back to India?

In the six months since I'd returned to the U.S., this thought had surfaced on a fairly regular basis. In spite of my best efforts, nothing had come close to the miracle of quitting smoking. But all that was about to change.

THERE IS NO STAGE V

New York City, 2007

A breeze blew through my open window. A freak October snowstorm had sparked the radiator to life and, though the day was warm, there was no turning down the heat.

I was at my desk scouring Nerve.com personals when in popped a Facebook message from Jenny, head of the yoga shala in Goa.

    Hi Lisa, would you be interested in
    coming to Goa this season?

Was this the wizardry of Gongyo Willy talked about?

    Funny,   I   was   just   looking   at
    flights.

I opened a new tab.

In her next message, Jenny explained she wanted someone to run her shop. Disappointed she didn't see me as teacher material, I decided to overlook the snub. The

121

pay was terrible and I'd have to fund my own travel, but the employment visa would allow me to stay in India for an entire year. Plenty of time to figure out what was still preventing me from making a love connection.

The first order of business was finding substitutes for my yoga classes. I wasn't about to give up my Manhattan address, or teaching. My big idea was to bring in people who could cover the four months I'd be employed at Jenny's shala. After scoring a tenant through Craigslist, I went about finding teaching subs. I also procured that visa—an experience that took me back to that train station in Mapusa—and plans started falling into place. I could worry about updating plans later. Maybe I wouldn't need to.

I was half under my bed when my cell phone rang, pushing boxes around to make space for items I planned to hide there while I was away. Ordinarily I'd have let the call go to voicemail, but I hoped it might be one of the yoga teachers I'd been trying to line up.

That I could walk away from this life, even temporarily, was a sign of radical growth. *Maybe*, I thought to myself as I scooted out from underneath my bed, *it's because I can finally feel my breath when I sit to meditate.*

Of late, I'd been able to sit for long, unstructured periods. During this time, I even had a lucid dreaming moment in the shower, where the skin fell from my bones in a reassuring premonition of sloughing off the mortal coil. I took it as a sign of my readiness—I'd never been so thoroughly prepared to transition from one phase to the next. I couldn't wait to get to India.

Brushing off a couple of dust bunnies, I took the two steps required to reach my "office." My sister's name appeared on my phone. In the middle of the workday.

"Mom has cancer," Tess said. "It's Stage IV lung and lymph."

"She what?" I asked but knew as if I'd been expecting the call. "How much time do we have?"

Tess clucked her tongue. "As if they'd tell me."

That our parents had told us even this much was mind-blowing. More than once, my father had driven himself to the emergency room. I only know about the times I happened to be living there. There's no telling how often he might have been his own ambulance jitney. In our house, sickness was weakness. We certainly never discussed ailments.

"Hang on," I said, and started looking up the prognosis for someone with Stage IV lung and lymph cancer. Mom might have six months, max. "Jesus Christ, there is no Stage V."

My whole life I'd wanted nothing more than to be on Mom's team. Besides referring to my sister as her "big girl" and "favorite," Mom often spent what felt like hours staring into Tess' face, popping zits while I looked on with envy. I had pimples too, but mine went disregarded. How I craved that attention.

Mom was my orbit.

There was a magic to her. When I was very young, I thought she might be a witch. She read palms, tarot, and knew about all the astrological signs. I asked her questions constantly, hoping she'd notice me.

"What does our horoscope say today?" Luckily we were both Libras.

"Let's see," she'd say, flipping through the paper. I liked to sit close enough to catch the scent of newsprint underneath the cigarettes.

Maybe that was why Mom started carting me—and only me, not my sister—along to her psychic readings. Though not the only fortune teller we saw, Miss Lorena's house was central to a number of Rust Belt towns, and over the years we often circled back to her.

During our back-to-back appointments, my mom usually went first. I'd wait on Miss Lorena's wagon-wheel patterned couch till it was my turn, then we'd switch places. Miss Lorena's office was in a small room, possibly a converted closet, dominated by a folding card table that held, yes, a crystal ball. Otherwise, Miss Lorena—doughy, with curly dark hair that fell to her shoulders, and, in my memory anyway, always in a velour tracksuit—looked far more like a suburban mom than my own mother, setting a credibility standard: the less psychic they tried to look, the more I believed in their abilities.

Though I enjoyed the adult feeling of having my own appointment, it was the post-consultation chats I lived for. This was as close as my mother ever came to doling out maternal advice.

"What did she tell you?" Mom would ask.

Though I remember very little of what she told me, I do recall one session clearly. "She saw two kids in my future." I looked at the cigarette smoke haloing my mother's head. "But they wouldn't be mine."

"Lucky," Mom said, staring straight out the windshield. "I wish I never had kids."

I was not shocked, nor did I feel hurt. I agreed with her; she'd have been better off without any of us. Whenever I saw women on TV like Mary Tyler Moore, or Marlo Thomas, or Carol Burnett, I thought the worlds they inhabited were far better suited to her than stay-at-home mom.

She hadn't been remiss as a mother, though her style could be described as pointed. Mom had taught me to read long before I started school, and also carted me to every art and dance class she could find wherever we moved. She'd even cooked me special meals to appease my finicky appetite. But she never made motherhood or wifery something aspirational.

The first time I baked something for her we were living in Greensburg—across from Robert F. Nicely Elementary—so I know I couldn't have been more than seven. After warming a concoction of flour and salt and water in the oven, I presented my mom with the muffin tin. She took one look and hissed at my father, "*Bob!* She's making cake."

The next toy I got was a microscope, which I cherished.

"You will grow up to be very successful," Miss Lorena augured on another visit; we were in Murrysville by then, so I was maybe thirteen.

By what magic? I wondered. My mother was much smarter and better-looking than anyone I'd ever met, yet she'd landed in a life she despised, following my father through the suburbs, her sole rebellion to delay acquiring her driver's license till she could no longer deny that she'd never reclaim an urban lifestyle.

Mom hated driving. Her foot hovered over the brake at all times. Often she had to pull over, causing my sister and me to roll our eyes across the car's bench seat. We didn't have the words "panic attack," only "drama queen."

By the time we moved to Murrysville, Mom had been driving about five years. The day we came home from school to find Mom's curiously sporty, 1969 Mercury Cougar coupe (Dad's purchase), but not our father's company car, I was sure a relocation announcement was imminent.

It was 1978. Murrysville's McMansions were just beginning to sprout. Tucked into the nape of the Allegheny mountains, we lived in an area unironically referred to as "Old Murrysville," a plot of modest starter homes built in the 1950s atop one of the town's significant inclines. Coming or going anywhere was like scaling the Matterhorn. Murrysville's single traffic light hung at the intersection where the bar and grocery store met. Having assimilated Mom's preference for a more cosmopolitan lifestyle, I was ready to leave.

Dad lined us all up on the living room's longer green-striped woolen couch, but I could barely sit still I was so excited. Soon I'd live in a different house, go to a new school, and have a fresh chance at recasting myself, preferably as someone more popular. Of course he was about to announce our next move, it was the only reason we ever had family meetings.

"Everybody." Dad paused for dramatic effect, ever the showman. "I'm buying a health club."

Prescient as it may seem now to have purchased a gym in 1979—just before the steel industry gasped its dying breath and Jane Fonda was about to make aerobics a household word—you should know there were people alive at that time who didn't don sweatbands. Namely, the people in my family. Besides Dad.

"Where?" my mother asked.

"In Holiday Park!" he said.

"Where's that?" my sister and I asked in unison.

"About two miles away."

Were we moving?

"We won't be moving."

"What!" the three of us demanded at once, but with entirely separate intentions.

Though usually we paired by color, the blonds against the brunettes, this time my dark-haired sister and blond dad were united in delight while Mom and I seethed. Tess, I understood. She wouldn't have to switch high schools again. But Mom?

At thirteen, I couldn't grasp the instability of starting a new business or the insult of getting the information at the same time as one's children. Then there was the new job she got as we all became Dad's hirees.

Gone were Mom's animal prints and outsized hats, replaced by jeans and oversized polo shirts emblazoned with the gym's logo. I can picture her now, perched at the reception desk, elbows propped on the glass counter, floating above pricey racquetball racquets and kidskin gloves.

"Your father knew I didn't like to exercise when he met me," she said one day, maybe a year into this business venture.

I crossed my arms and looked at the parking lot through the front window. "Why don't you leave him?" I asked, fangirling the flames of her anger. Commiseration was the closest I could get to her then.

She took a long last drag off her Kent. "And do what?" She stabbed at the ashtray beside her.

I'd built my life in opposition to her passivity, determined I'd never be trapped. Now Stage IV lung and lymph cancer? *Oh, Mom.*

"I have to cancel India," I told my sister. Of the two of us, I was the logical choice. Tess lived in D.C., where she had a full-time office job. "Go to Mom and Dad's."

"You're going to stay at their house?" Neither of us thought of the place as home. She'd lived there less time than I had. "Or in your duplex?"

Though I'd kept my place, in part for that far-off unimaginable future in which my parents were old and infirm, now was not that time, surely. Besides, both units were rented out, and I needed the income.

"Yes. I'm going to stay at their house. I know it's not a great idea, but it's what I've got."

Soon as we hung up, I composed a resignation letter to Jenny; I hadn't begun so it wasn't quitting so much as not showing up. I despaired of leaving her in the lurch, but missing our family's last Christmas together would've been irredeemable. I hit send before I could second-guess.

SHOES GO ON THE TABLE

Murrysville, 2007

Though my mother quit smoking after my sister and I left for college, I still recall the Murrysville house in a haze of smoke, and dark. And while often the sky was gray—at least three hundred days out of the year—my memory is as emotional as visual. Murrysville was when kids my age started drinking.

Though I'd been drinking in secret since Bay City—either stealing shots from my parents' liquor cabinet or while on the job as a babysitter—now my antics were public.

"Kirchner, do you know what you did last night?" was a refrain I found only mildly less humiliating than, "You alkie!" I'd read *Go Ask Alice*. I knew alcoholics weren't supposed to drink. But to my fifteen-year-old ears, not drinking sounded like a fate worse than death.

Two excruciating years later, when my sophomore

year ended yet we were still in Murrysville, Dad assigned me split shifts: Monday through Friday, eight to eleven and six to eleven. So much for my summer break.

Less than two weeks into this schedule, my partying got in the way of my hours. "Come on, lazybones," Dad yelled into my bedroom.

Did he yell? My head was pounding. Lying in bed to keep the world from toppling on its axis, I wondered why I'd painted the ceiling the same sky-blue as my walls. I rolled over and moaned, "I don't feel well. I'm not coming."

Suddenly Dad was in my room. The air had to have been heavy with the stink of unmetabolized alcohol and cigarettes. Even he couldn't ignore this evidence.

"You're a disgrace." He was definitely yelling. "You're ruining your life. You're never going to amount to anything. You disgust me."

He slammed the door on the way out, but thanks to the vagaries of architecture, the door didn't shut but puffed back open. Fury licked at my insides as I rose to close it, pulling the hallway phone into my room.

Mark answered on the first ring. "Fuck you."

This was before caller ID, and though Mark had left me at the end of our driveway merely two hours before to sneak back into my house through the sliders, I knew he'd answer. He had his own phone.

"My dad is such an asshole," I started right in too. "Why do I have to work all summer?"

"That sucks."

"I hate my life. I can't take it," I whined. "Let's go to West Virginia today and get shitfaced."

West Virginia, the next state over, was our go-to place for partying. The drinking age there was only eighteen, which made Mark legal.

"Fuck that," Mark said.

My heart sank.

Mark and I weren't lovers and never would be—I was a fifteen-year-old virgin without a driver's license—but he was into me. Between having money, a car, and a crush, he'd always been willing to drive the hour and a half it took to get to Wheeling. If he tired of me, I was screwed.

"Let's go to California," he said. "I have an aunt there who'll put us up."

Our plan was hatched. I loaded up three garbage bags, and together we drove across the country to California. We camped and thieved and continued our sexless relationship all the way across the country, where we did meet up with his aunt. But eventually, summer ended.

When I tried to enroll in the local high school, my parents refused to release my transcripts. I couldn't afford to hire an attorney to be legally emancipated and so, faced with the prospect of getting a GED—which to me meant never getting into college—I skulked home. My family never discussed the matter, but I did go out and get a new job busing tables at Dick's Diner.

I didn't see the pain I caused or the kindnesses I received, or even my reckless behavior. I was only aware how much I hurt. The rest of high school went by in a blur.

"Kirchner, are you always high?" the captain of our school's football team asked during junior or maybe senior year. Not that the year makes any difference. The answer was yes.

Revisiting Murrysville was hardly appealing.

Mom started chemo even before I got to the house. Prepared as I thought I was to see her, I was not. She'd lost weight and had a pallor, but it was her hair that shocked me. Only tufts remained, dotting her head. Why had no one cut it? She'd forever been vain about her locks, making this un-seeing all the more heartbreaking.

I chopped and shaved what remained on her scalp. "Even the shape of your head is beautiful," I told her because it was.

There was no crying or hugging or soul-searching conversation—we did what we did best. "Check this one out," I said, pointing at a sparkly purple turban in a website storefront. "You could start charging to read people's fortunes!"

We purchased a few exotic turbans and some wigs that mimicked her natural head of hair—now silver with black streaks—but never returned to psychics or predictions of any sort. Instead, Mom burrowed into her Catholicism, Saints' Days and prayer cards replacing horoscopes and Tarot. The future had lost its appeal.

My father and sister, I resented. Why had they neglected mom?

One night the four of us were in the family room watching television when Tess reached for my dad's shoes from where he'd placed them on the coffee table, a massive sliver of cypress we'd sealed and filled with seashells while watching the Steelers third Super Bowl win. When her hand gripped the beige leather, I found my mother's eyes across the room. Nothing good could come of this. Sure enough, she moved his soft-soled loafers to the floor.

As long as I'd known my father, the man stayed fully dressed until he went to bed. This included his shoes. Other than pool- or oceanside, I'd never seen his feet bare or his footgear lying idle, let alone *on* the coffee table. Surely he had his reasons for flouting conventions of coffee table and stockinged feet etiquette, reasons that were not to be discussed.

I was not surprised when Dad put his shoes right back where they'd been. I was, however, astonished when Tess returned them to the floor.

Dad moved them back.

This went on for several rounds before words were exchanged. "Leave my things where I put them, goddammit!"

To my amazement, my sister grabbed his footwear *again*.

"Shoes go on the floor!"

Suddenly Dad and Tess each had a hold of the shoes, wrestling them back and forth as their argument escalated. Mom and I sat watching in stunned silence. Dad yelled, "Get out and don't come back." And she did. For months.

That this happened while my mother was in treatment for Stage IV lung and lymph cancer horrified even me, a member of this small, dysfunctional family unit. Though banished from the house by my father, Mom and Tess continued speaking by telephone. Eventually the ban was lifted, but I was long gone having left shortly after this fight, before Mom's treatment ended.

Expecting I'd need to return to my parents' home soon, I shortened my work leave, returning to Sophia's apartment while she was still away on break. Once back in Manhattan, I vowed to call my mom every day, wanting to share whatever *now* we had left.

I also went back to therapy.

BIG LOVE

New York City, 2008-2009

"I had a vision of a raven plucking the disease from my lungs," Mom told me over the phone, her way of explaining she was free of cancer.

She didn't elaborate, and I didn't ask, certain her prognosis wouldn't hold up to scrutiny. Though no longer worried I was on the verge of drug and alcohol relapse, Mom's imminent death reminded me, if my dating life kept on like this, when my time came I wouldn't have anyone.

Do I only have twenty-five years left? Or less?

"What would happen if parents ran out of love after one child?" Ricky asked, staring directly into my eyes.

We were at a bar on the Upper East Side—unlike being around weed, I'd never minded being in pubs so long as I had a reason to be there besides watching other people drink. Though the establishment was near where I taught yoga, Ricky wasn't my student exactly. We'd met in a class I was subbing. Of course I'd noticed him. Between his dark eyes and pale complexion, Ricky had the brooding look of a silent film star. When he posed his question, I could offer only a wide-eyed silence in response.

Does he want kids? Is he open to adoption?

"The human capacity for love is boundless," Ricky went on.

Maybe I won't die alone.

"Otherwise, we'd never have evolved."

I had no idea where Ricky was going with his spiel, but I was glad to be along for the ride. Though flirtatious and chatty around class, he'd never taken the interactions any farther. So I did. In the name of research for an article, I asked him to tell me his best vacation sex story. He'd invited me to listen. Over a drink. *Bingo.*

"I've been wanting to talk to you," Ricky said. "But I wasn't sure if it was OK."

"It's fine," I said, assuming he meant the taboo of crossing the student/teacher line. "You aren't in my regular class."

Ricky furrowed his brow but went on to profess his interest. In my writing. He and his partner organized adult parties. Maybe I'd write one up. *Partner? Adult?* Were those euphemisms for wife and sex? The answers were yes.

Before my marriage, I equated multiple sex partners with cheating. Not so much since the unwanted split.

Maybe the years of living in the polygamous Muslim land of Qatar had softened me to the idea, but keeping all the wives around now struck me as far gentler than discarding them.

"Maybe we should see other people but stay married?" I'd asked my ex in our single in-person meeting. A desperate leap, to be sure, but he had to be at least as bored by our sex life as I was.

My then still-husband's olive skin went uncharacteristically pink, or perhaps the color was more obvious against those green-striped couches. He merely shook his head in response. *No.*

Now here was this Ricky, a person I'd met in the real world, freely discussing his spouse and their active celebration of many lovers.

"You want me to write an article about your sex parties?"

"Oh, no." He smiled. "Our parties are about much more than sex. You don't need to remove so much as a wristwatch."

As I wondered how I'd come across as uptight, Ricky explained that he and his wife didn't host swingers' parties because they were polyamorists. Their get-togethers were about more than sex, he said, because polyamory embraced an expanded definition of love, one that included multiple partners. "It's about the possibilities of our emotional landscape," he said. "It *is* possible to love more than one person at a time, deeply and intimately."

His words rang true.

My feelings for Jeffrey, my first love, hadn't died with him. Yet I'd gone on to meet and marry another. In much the same way, the ex's disappearance didn't flip an emotional off-switch. In the world I wanted to inhabit, recovering from lost love meant learning to live with loss, not scorning the love that existed.

If I hoped to marry again, I was going to have to start somewhere. Like a modern-day Margaret Mead, I would study Ricky. He had a wife and multiple other female companions. I could observe the group up close, familiarize myself with their mating behavior. Once I'd learned their ways, I could adopt them and join their ranks, becoming someone whose heart was "boundless." Surely, I would find love.

I took more direct aim.

"You're just so... attentive." I smiled, blinking as if bewildered. "I thought you were attracted to me." *Now look away.*

"Oh, but I am attracted to you," he said. "I wanted you to know about my situation first."

Perfect.

"I'm single and childless and live in Manhattan," I told Adrienne, the therapist I'd contacted at Willy's behest. "My mom's life work has come to fruition."

Adrienne wrinkled her high, otherwise smooth brow. "How does that thought feel?"

Adrienne worked at the Blanton Peale Institute, a teaching center Willy had told me about. "You can afford it," he'd insisted. "They have a sliding scale."

I put off reaching out for months, till Mom was diagnosed with cancer. Not only was Willy right about the pricing, it turned out that their office was between my apartment and a yoga class I taught several times a week, and right across from my favorite coffee shop. The only excuse I had left was the affiliation. The Peale in question was Norman Vincent, he of *The Power of Positive Thinking*. If Adrienne came at me with an affirmation, I was ready to walk out. So far she hadn't, but asking how my thoughts felt diminished my trust. So basic.

"It feels accurate."

"But is it really true?"

Now I furrowed my brow. What did this lady want from me?

"Or okay, say you're right," Adrienne continued. "How does that thought serve you?"

I hadn't decided if I was going to keep our second appointment.

Ricky's courtship began slowly, regular dating. Dinner. Theater. A day at Coney Island. This meshed well with my evolving philosophy, that I should want to wake up with someone before I went to bed with them.

For Ricky, the circumstances were different. He had to coordinate with his wife's dating schedule—she'd started seeing someone new but they'd not yet consummated their relationship. We weren't allowed go there until they did.

While I could appreciate the lack of affectation, there was an assumption behind it that made for a disconcerting leap. Though relatively chaste, the careful coordination presumed the relationship would evolve. Then one afternoon, Ricky sent an IM about meeting his wife. Was he hoping we'd hit it off? I responded quickly:

`What for?`

For some bizarre reason I harbored the belief that group sex was a hidden agenda item, one I'd be required to participate in if I planned to hang with this crowd for long. My brain had gone right to this suspicion. The idea of sex with a woman wasn't the issue, it was the group angle of group sex I didn't like. Much as I'd grown accustomed to the idea of being relegated to a lower tier in a lover's life, in the heat of passion, I wanted to be the priority.

`To meet?` Ricky texted back.

I wondered about that question mark, but before I replied more words appeared on the screen.

`Before the party.`

The adult party I hadn't written about.

Again, he wrote back before I answered.

`She likes to know who my girlfriends are, so we can discuss boundaries.`

Girlfriend?

`Boundaries?` I replied, wondering if I shouldn't feel more excited about being called his girlfriend. Wasn't that what I'd wanted?

`What we are and aren't allowed to do, so there aren't any surprises.`

Allowed to do? She's going to have some say in... what? Our sex positions?

`The party shouldn't be the first time you meet.`

`God forbid I come on to her.` When Ricky

didn't reply, I added, `LOL`.

This shorthand was meant to suggest I was cool with all this, which, evidently and increasingly, I was not. Had he actually known me, Ricky would've known how much I loathed that acronym.

His messaging dots appeared.

`Come on to her?`

Didn't he see the LOL? What to say now?

More dots. Ricky had barely begun.

`I don't want you having sex with anyone at the party.`

WHAT.

Ricky had his wife *and* other lovers. All I had were intermittent bouts with him, and I had yet to get laid at all. What did it matter if I met someone at his party? More to the point, if I did, what could he do to stop me?

In reality, when I thought about the party, I lurched between fantasies of hooking up with a stranger and sneaking out the nearest exit. I *was* squeamish. I wasn't a swinger trying to disguise myself as a polyamorist, I wanted just one person to commit to. Not that I judged Ricky's choices, but they weren't for me.

Then again, wasn't I on a mission? I might learn more from her. What kind of wizard was she to wield the power to keep a reverse harem going? Maybe I should date her.

`Of course I'll meet your wife.`

"Has this pattern been activated in other relationships?" Adrienne asked at our second session. Ricky hadn't come up yet.

"Well, I was never married before so no one has ever had the chance to—"

"What I mean is," she said, her foot bouncing at the end of her crossed leg.

Classic inexperience, I thought, reading her body language as impatience. No therapist who was any good would be this affordable.

"Have you experienced anything that felt similar to this situation? With any other person?"

Also no. *Duh.* My inability to form a new relationship was the whole reason I'd returned to therapy. Was she not listening?

It's a wonder I held out hope for love. My anthropological investigation had thus far been limited to my interactions with Ricky, which wasn't helping. And then came the day all that assuming came to pass.

Ricky texted from the road. We'd gotten the okay to bone. What I discovered in that moment was that without any pretense, the tension was lacking. There was no frisson, only a bit of panic.

`Pick up some coconut oil.`

Some what? Coconut oil was not yet in the zeitgeist as an edible wonder lubricant/cure-all. I had no idea what he wanted and the only thing approximating coconut oil at the pharmacy nearest my house was meant for hair. Skeptical this was the way to go but eager for the unknown pleasures ahead, I snapped up my prize and scampered home.

He didn't say, but right away, I knew the hair oil was a disappointment. We plowed ahead. As Ricky plotted a course through my erogenous zones, I got the impression that this was his pattern. Like I was a numbered canvas to which he was applying paint. Maybe this explained why the wife was willing to lend him out.

When it was over Ricky announced he was up to twenty partners. "One more, and I'm legal." He grinned.

"Now?" I asked. "As in concurrently?"

"No, total."

He was pretty excited about his number, so I kept my mouth shut. My count exceeded his and winning a numbers game wasn't something I'd ever aimed for, or viewed as an accomplishment. Just math. I had a good ten years on Ricky and I'd been single most of my adult life.

I longed to take heart in the fact that, even after our consummation, we still went on dates. But Ricky and I had different ideas of fun.

On the afternoon of a predetermined date night, Ricky called to ask if I'd like to go out for falafel then a giant puppet festival. I couldn't imagine any two activities I'd rather do less, separately. Combining them would be uniquely dreadful.

"I'm not feeling the falafel, Ricky, I'm gonna pass on tonight," I told him, proud I'd articulated any preference. His response was a shock.

"You're so controlling. You don't want to do anything you don't think of!"

Because I didn't like fried dough? Or boredom? As far as I was concerned, puppetry was one level below clowns on the entertainment scale. But the tone in his voice made it sound as if we'd been having this argument for years. We'd barely been seeing each other for two months.

"I'm sorry," I lied, wondering if he was right. "I'm not feeling well."

We hung up but I couldn't shake the conversation. Was I too controlling? Ricky dictated who I could and couldn't have sex with, how, and where we had sex. Who was controlling whom?

To my surprise, a wedge of enthusiasm surfaced. Judging my feelings was my problem, the way I'd muddied my sense of self. I had to call Willy right away.

"That slogan—feelings aren't facts—it's bullshit," I said.

"You think your feelings are the truth?" he asked.

"I do," I said. "It's how I think about my feelings that gives me trouble. If I don't feel like watching giant puppets, that's the truth. That doesn't make my feelings right, Ricky fucking loves a giant puppet. But telling myself how I feel is wrong? That's denial."

"Thoughts are definitely liars."

When we got off the phone I decided to sit and meditate. Goenka had said that agitation in the body was a manifestation of agitation in the mind, so I'd been trying to pinpoint where in my body my emotional pains lived, with the idea I'd tease them free with yoga poses. "Control issues" felt lodged in my solar plexus, right below "hopelessly single," perfect neurotic companions suggesting more backbends were needed.

A week before the adult party I had yet to write about, Ricky announced they were canceling. A burlesque convention that same weekend had siphoned off too much of their audience. As consolation, he suggested we spend the weekend together.

The whole weekend? His time may have suddenly freed up, but mine hadn't.

Confronted by these feelings, I could no longer deny the truth—a married man wanted more than I was willing to give. This wasn't working. I messaged Ricky.

`Can you get together this after-`
`noon?`

But Ricky was busy.

`Tomorrow?`

`I'll see you Friday when I pick you`
`up.`

Good Christ, no. I had to end this before then.

`I don't think we should see each`
`other.`

There was more to our exchange, including anger that I'd do such a thing by text, but Ricky's finest line was this:

`You're better off being in a`
`relationship than alone and unhappy.`

It was precisely what I needed to hear. If I was going to be unhappy, I wanted to be solely responsible.

Was this spiritual or selfish? I wondered.

What would Willy do?

MR. RIGHT NOW

New York City, 2009-2010

I needed Willy's opinion but couldn't reach him. Luckily, he was at the noon meeting.

Though it was early summer still, the day was sticky. After the meeting, we grabbed iced coffees and headed into the green blaze of Tompkins Square Park.

"Thanks for making the time, I—" My voice cracked and the tears started to spill before I'd even begun my story. After ending things with Ricky, I'd messaged Keith.

Eventually I squeaked it out, how, after sleeping together again, my former writing teacher once more made plain that we were barely fuck buddies. We had common friends and interests. We shared similar goals.

"How is it that he doesn't see us together?" I asked, as if Willy would know. *What is so hideous about me?*

My melancholy momentarily spent, I looked into the

dog run, visible just beyond our bench. *I miss my dogs!* "I wish we could work it out like dogs do."

"You wanna leave a turd at Keith's door?"

Thank God for Willy. "Yes, *and...*" My new favorite phrase. Recently, thinking I'd signed up for sketch writing, I'd landed in an improv class. I would've righted the mistake, but it turned out I loved improv. Also, no homework. "I do wish I could find someone."

"But you *can*," he said. "No point in skipping over Mr. Right Now while you're waiting for Mr. Right."

This again?

A few months earlier, after listening to my complaints about Ricky, Willy had introduced me to yet another world of online dating. Sitting before his enormous computer monitor, my spiritual mentor typed a few strokes and, to my befuddlement, pulled up an adult website.

"Oof, Willy, didn't we just learn I'm not cut out for orgies?"

"Girl, what are you talking about? There's a whole world of options. Look, casual sex is a category."

"Casual sex? Who said anything about casual sex?"

"Oh stop it right now. Between all your teaching jobs and your mom on death's door, writing that book and going to therapy and meetings, do you really think you have time for a relationship?"

He had me there.

Ever since my mother's death had become imminent, I'd stopped wishing for the release of oncoming traffic, craving purchase instead. Squandering my time and attention with prospects uninterested in relationships had felt like a distraction. Then I'd met Ricky.

Much as I feared being adrift, the idea of being anchored was worse. If I'd learned anything from the inchoate feelings that regularly surfaced during my yoga practice, it was that my body was a storehouse of emotions. What if carnal exploration was a way to go deeper? What deeper place was there than actually inside my body?

Willy was still talking. "It's not like you can get it wrong."

"I can't?"

Willy's suggestion was starting to sound more like taking improv instead of sketch writing. Less homework. Less work.

"That sounds fucking amazing."

"Come on," Willy said, standing. "Let's go write your profile."

I don't know which of us was more surprised when I agreed. Willy practically ran me up the five flights of steps it took to get to his apartment.

A resident of Alphabet City since the days of stepping over junkies, Willy had a proper, rent-controlled one-bedroom with a living room, a dining room, and an eat-in kitchen. His desk—a piece of wood laid over sawhorses—ran the length of his entire living room wall, enough space for his mixing board, monitor, and both of us. He often recorded vocals in his flat. I pulled up a chair, and we got to work.

"They don't care about the words," he laughed as I agonized over my verbiage. "Just the pictures. Don't you have anything sexier?"

Finally, Willy approved a shot that was, I hoped, unrecognizable—my back, shoulders to butt, with my hands slicing the center in a reverse namaste. Thank the gods this site didn't require a face pic.

Because we were both creatives, and because he hadn't dumped me for not pursuing Goju Kai (though occasionally I still accompanied him to chant, loath to, in recovery-speak, "miss the miracle"), I trusted him as much as I trusted anyone.

"Ooh! Say how big you want his dick to be."

"What? No! You're the size queen, not me," I laughed.

But Willy wasn't joking. "Why not ask for exactly what you want?"

"Here's what *I* wrote." I read from the screen. "Let's not waste time. Let's meet for coffee, hook up if we feel like it, and if it's any good, maybe we'll do it again. I don't need to meet your mother, but I'm nobody's secret."

"Good," he said. "But they're just looking at your pictures."

"Well, at least I'm being clear. The last thing I need to add to my resume is *homewrecker*."

"You don't believe that, do you?" Willy asked.

"I don't think marriages break up because someone cheats, that's just a symptom." I'd never wondered if my ex had cheated; even if he had, I wouldn't have considered that the primary problem. "But if someone is cheating, there's gonna be drama. Oh, that reminds me."

I typed. "No training/no drama."

"That's good."

"Do you think you're going to get it right this time?" Adrienne asked when I told her what had happened with Keith, tightening a shawl around her shoulders, the August heat not making a dent in her meat locker of an office. Six months in and I knew the room's seasons, we overheated in the winter and froze in the summer.

"He's nothing like my ex," I replied, sipping the hot coffee I'd brought as my heat source. "My ex had no clue how attractive he was."

Keith had no such dilemma. The first time I ever saw him outside of class was at his apartment, where he'd invited all the students to attend his birthday soirée and, I assumed, show off his Upper West Side apartment with the skyline view. That night I'd watched, speechless, as female party-goers swarmed him. I'd been bewildered he chose me.

"I didn't say anything about your ex," Adrienne said.

She could be so aggravating.

My new dating profile changed everything. As I met men with no expectation of anything other than possibly sex, there was no bullshit.

Forget about what I wrote on my profile about wanting a relationship. You described exactly what I'm looking for.

He was responding to what I'd written?

I made a mental note to tell Willy and deleted the

message. With all my cards face up and on the table, I had no tolerance for subterfuge.

Astoundingly, I began seeing men on a somewhat regular basis. Men with whom I communicated beyond, "U up?" Had it been so simple all along, that honesty began with being true to myself? Unlike with Ricky— where our behavior was predetermined—nothing about these connections could be taken for granted.

We went out to dinner, to shows, and theater. Sure, there was sex aplenty. But these men were also there for me, helping, at various times, paint my apartment, review legal contracts, and assemble Ikea furniture. Fucking heroes, all. This was working.

"You'll never believe this," I said to Adrienne. "Somebody recognized my ex in an essay."

I should not have been surprised when she didn't respond, but I wanted to know her thoughts. "Isn't that horrifying?"

"Is that how you'd describe it?"

Didn't I just?

"I guess I didn't tell you the worst part," I said, poking at the ice in my coffee cup to free a few last swigs.

"Have you ever noticed how you do that?"

"Do what?"

"Every time something difficult comes up, you take a drink," she said. "You use that coffee as an emotional buffer."

"Well I guess that's how I landed in rehab at nineteen." I shook my head. This was a big deal I was trying to talk about. "Anyway, this troll apparently *knew* him. Said he was a great guy.

"So I commented, 'I couldn't agree more, that's why I married him.' Then all these other people started piling on, suggesting she must've had an affair with him. Total insanity!"

"Is it?"

"Other people have suggested that, but I never thought so. Even if he did, what do I care? I was the one who suggested we should sleep with other people in the first place."

"You've mentioned that." Excruciating pause.

I broke the silence. "And?"

"Well you've also said that with Ricky, you realized you weren't interested in polyamory."

Now it was my turn to be silent.

"What are you feeling?"

"I don't know," I said.

"Can you breathe into the discomfort, give it some room?"

"Of course I can breathe into it," I said, not pausing to take that breath. "I am a goddamn yoga teacher."

"Do you remember that doctor from Match?" I asked my mom in one of our daily calls. I hadn't mentioned the adult website to Mom, we weren't *that* kind of tight. "We met up yesterday. He was on his phone the entire time we were together."

"Did you tell him you have a sick mother? Maybe he has contacts in Pittsburgh."

Even for her it was a land speed record for hijacking a story.

"Mom," I said sharply, then took a deep breath. Adrienne would be proud. "Gosh I just saw the time, I have to run. I'm meeting Willy. Call you tomorrow!"

"Don't go to the hardware store for apples," Willy said when I relayed the story over chicken tagine platters at a Moroccan restaurant between our apartments.

Nodding, I slowed my chewing, savoring the tangy flavors. I'd heard this expression in meetings many times, but only now did I see how it applied, how I'd been ignoring what I'd long known about my mother—she never wanted kids.

Mom was the eldest of seven, eight if you included the stillborn sibling, which my mom did. According to her, the baby's death threw Grandma into a depression, leaving my mother to pick up the slack around the house. As far as Mom was concerned, the whole of her life had been consumed by child care. I wonder if she'd ever fully experienced childhood.

What she wanted now was to be taken care of. I understood, how could I not? Hadn't I once craved nurturing so badly I'd signed myself into a psych ward on campus, Upham Hall?

Keith messaged me. Yes, he was still in the picture; such a hard drug to quit. But no, this wasn't a booty call. Once more, he wanted to let me know he was getting back with his kinda sorta girlfriend.

`Okay, I'm heading back to Qatar soon`

anyway.

Message dots appeared. Ha!

That's terrific.

Fucker. But I'd show him how little he meant to me. I would never write about him either.

THAT'S TERRIFIC!

New York City, 2010-2011

Telling Keith I was moving to Qatar wasn't just a smoke screen. A friend forwarded the job announcement months ago:

Did you see, the Tribeca Film Festival is looking for a marketing director? In Qatar??? You should apply!!

Though I'd clicked on the attached application, I'd thought little more about it. I'd never worked in film. When they offered the job, I was shocked.

The idea of returning to the site of my heartbreak was not particularly appealing, but three years had elapsed since I'd left. I needed to finish my book about Qatar, and the financial package would help. Besides, returning might make for a nice epilogue. Or that's how I was trying to sell it to Willy as I pedaled toward the

Vanderbilt Y.

"Maybe it's a chance to see if I've learned whatever lesson I was supposed to get," I said through my headset.

"You know you don't have to go anywhere to transform suffering into joy, right?"

I'd heard as much, but I couldn't see how staying in one place had ever done much for me, either. Travel, on the other hand, had turned me into a non-smoker (a miracle I still held close), a yoga teacher, and, I hoped, an author.

Doubts played like a drumbeat throughout the class.

"Inhale." *If I never ran away from home, I'd never have gotten sober.*

"Exhale." *Then again, joining the Peace Corps hadn't turned out so well.*

"Less effort!" *Maybe I shouldn't take the job in Qatar?*

After class I raced home to call Mom before Dad got home from the gym, a feat made easier by my new bike.

I never thought of myself as a cyclist, but the Trek hybrid I'd heaved around since 1994 had been a huge part of my life. Until the day I met the Indian saint, Amma, a.k.a, "The Hugging Mama." When I emerged from the Manhattan Center in a post-hug daze, I circumnavigated the entire block twice before concluding that—after three years of living on the streets of Manhattan—my bike had finally been stolen.

Not only would I fail to make it on time to the patchwork of classes I taught if I relied on public transit, I couldn't take the hit to my budget. I went straight to Kmart and bought another. Luckily for me, a paramour—

after one look at the heavy and impractical model I'd purchased based on its attractive price—gifted me a fully un-restored, circa 1982 Bianchi road bike.

"She's been through a lot," he said, running his palm across the bike's rusting and dinged frame. "Like you. But she works perfectly." *Did he mean my psyche or my face?* Soon enough, I didn't care. Bianca, as I called her, was much faster than the Trek.

These thoughts crossed my mind in a flash as I quickly locked her up; Mom didn't like it when I called from the road—"you're too distracted"—so I waited to ring her with the news till I got into my apartment.

"I'll be starting another round of chemo by the time you leave for Qatar," Mom said.

"What?" I peeled off my bag and jacket. "Should I not go?"

"Of course you should go," she said. "I'm fine. It's just another round of chemo. The radiation was much worse."

Unlike her story about the bird plucking cancer from her lungs, this assertion I could question. The hideousness of chemo was universally acknowledged. "How is that possible?"

"The treatment's really advanced, hon. Oh, there's the garage door. I better start dinner. But you should go."

I checked my watch; plenty of time to fact-check her assertion before my next class. But I didn't.

When I fired up my computer at home I found—to my horror—an email from my ex. After years without contact, he'd responded to my email.

Though I'd rejected Adrienne's advice, the essay I'd

told her about had led to finding an agent. The agent said the same thing, suggesting that telling my ex would eventually be necessary to clear the path for publishing. Though my memoir wasn't about my ex, he was certainly in it. So I'd capitulated, writing a note as a courtesy. He knew I was writing about Qatar, we'd talked about it often, envisioning we'd one day be like the journalist couple Geraldine Brooks and Tony Horowitz, both of whom had written about living in the Arab world. I never expected to hear back; this was a man I'd had to chase in order to pay him his share of retirement funds.

"I was not aware you were writing a book," began his email.

I pushed back from my computer and looked out my window. *Not aware?* Had he forgotten our many conversations or just never taken me seriously? Rolling back to my terminal, I read on.

"I think that's terrific."

Terrific? He might as well have said nice.

"I am not worried how I might be portrayed."

Really?

He went on to describe how he was living by a lake with a woman and that they were about to adopt a child. His words seized my torso like a pair of white-hot tongs. My lungs collapsed, forgetting or unable to suck in air. This was the very life we'd often discussed. Only, I'd been replaced.

But the kicker was what got me.

He reported that Grandpa, our dog, had died in his "loving" arms. He'd not been able to find it in his heart to get another dog.

It was not mindfulness or restraint that stayed immediate response, but horror. Though I managed the three
steps it took to get to my bed, it was only to lie face down
and hyperventilate into a pillow.

One of the first things I'd discovered about life in
Doha was that dogs were considered haram, unclean
according to the Koran. Canines found wandering the
streets were as likely to be shot on sight as rounded up
and taken to a pound.

Our boys, Little Bear and Grandpa, ten and eight
respectively, liked to run off. If their wandering ways
didn't get them killed, the desert climate or rigorous
travel—twelve hours in the cargo hold of a plane—just
might. It seemed wisest to leave them with a friend for the
duration of this temporary assignment.

It did not take long to recognize my error. What was
home without the click clack of paws? The cool wet of a
furry nuzzle? When I met other expats who'd brought
their dogs, I insisted we retrieve our boys. The process
was unwieldy.

Organizing their vaccinations remotely was not overly
burdensome, but providing proof of breed was. I had to
interview various vets till I could find one willing to
claim that our big black furry mutts were Golden
Retriever mixes.

We'd not yet made it out of Pennsylvania before
border control at the Philadelphia airport stopped us.
"These guys are chipped, yeah?"

I didn't even know what that meant. Once it was

explained that without an identifying microchip the dogs would be "destroyed" on arrival in Qatar, we jumped out of line, booked a hotel that would take us and our two giant dogs for the night, found a vet willing to squeeze us into his schedule, and got them chipped. When at last we landed in Doha, the lack of dog culture worked in our favor. Having no idea what the various breeds should look like, no one questioned our boys' lineage.

Having the boys with us improved life dramatically in Qatar. Our enormous villa felt less like a pit stop between work shifts. Their snuggles made life manageable, and we even found time to take them running on Doha's wild beaches, the ones beyond the touristic development. Then one day Little Bear dashed out the front door while I was putting away groceries.

My worst fear had come true. And it was my fault.

While I printed and posted fliers and ran off to every sighting, my beloved fell into inaction. This was worse than anger. There was a history of paternal suicides in his family. My searching grew more frantic.

"She is very skinny, yes?" asked a compound guard.

"Skinny?" The thought of a slim Little Bear was horrid, but how would he fend for himself on the mean streets of Doha? He was accustomed to regular meals, and between those, hand-fed scraps of cheese. "Never mind. My dog is a *he*. Male dog."

"Yes, *he*. Brown, yes?"

"He's more black actually."

"Yes! Black! Come quickly."

"That description though…" I trailed off.

He texted the address. Across the conference table—I

was at work, stuffing gift bags for an event—my American colleague urged me to follow up.

At the compound I found a frail, damaged girl. But she approached, slowly, head down, nuzzling her snout into my palm. Her owner had to be looking for her, so I did what I hoped someone else had done already for Little Bear—I scooped her into my car and took her to the vet. She became our dog.

My husband was mortally offended by her presence. Grandpa, on the other hand, was beside himself with joy. He went from chewing everything in sight to following our new addition everywhere. When at last we named her Sophie "Ma Barker" Maslov, I told myself my husband had relented.

Until he left and stopped responding to my messages.

I doubt I'd have tried to force my soon-to-be ex-husband's hand, except we were supposed to meet for a lovers' rendezvous I'd tacked onto a business trip not ten days after he'd made the marriage-ending phone call. Through sheer will and magic—I'd heard horror stories of expats having to leave their dogs behind because of the paperwork—I arranged to take our pups back to the U.S. with me.

Still, he didn't respond. So, from the terminal, while trying to navigate two enormous dog crates, my luggage, and myself, I took the nuclear option and called his mother. That's how the hour long conversation about ending our marriage came about, after which he had to peel Grandpa off my parents' striped woolen couch. It was up to me to find a new home for Sophie, which I did (a farm where she could run as much as she liked).

Now, three years later, my ex had written to let me know how handily he'd switched me out. But Grandpa, the dog he'd tried to ignore? Him, he couldn't bear to replace?

Once some of the shock had worn off, the most damning aspect of this exchange settled in my bones—my ex's absolute lack of malice. Over the last three years, that man had spent far less time thinking about me than I had him.

Time! I had a class to teach.

I sat up, scrambling to find my phone in the bed. My stomach lurched. I had to leave.

The tears flowed as I tore across 12th Street, pedaling recklessly.

How can I still be so easily crushed by him? Devastation on top of devastation.

I made it to Chelsea Piers where I somehow managed to stop crying. This was a *restorative* class, no distractions. Just me, in my most calming voice, exhorting students to breathe through the discomfort of stillness.

After class, one of my long-time students, John, a retired city electrician, came up to talk. I braced myself, certain he was about to complain in his often-gruff manner. "Dat," he said in his thick Brooklyn accent, "was one of the best sessions you eva taught."

Trying to hide my shock, I thanked him and got the hell out of there. The journey home was a weepy repeat. I wondered which was worse—how I felt or how well I kept it hidden.

I booked an emergency session with Adrienne.

"Will I ever get better?" I asked her after I'd explained my dilemma.

"It depends on how willing you become to let someone hurt you."

I might've argued that my ex had hurt me enough, or some other defense, but Adrienne kept talking.

She said she'd seen progress, but also that I'd stalled. I might do better with another therapist.

She was breaking up with me?

Then she let me have it—Adrienne was pregnant and leaving the practice. Did I have any feelings about that?

Mostly just, *FUCK!* I was supposed to be leaving for Qatar in a few weeks. Not surprisingly, Adrienne wasn't offering Skype sessions during her maternity leave. And there wasn't time to start anew with another therapist in her practice. What now?

Riding home from our appointment—slowly now but still in tears—Elaine's words floated into my consciousness. "The answer is always more spirituality."

HONK!

A truck had veered perilously close. To my relief, I didn't want to turn into its steel fender. But I didn't want to live like this either.

THE KISS OF AYAHUASCA

New York City, 2011-2012

Not long before getting the ex's email I'd passed a friend on the street I didn't recognize.

"Hey, Lisa," I heard.

I had to do a double take. Who was that smiley guy?

"Brian?" Prior to this sighting, glum would've been the word I'd have used to describe Brian. This person was glowing. "Wow, you look amazing!"

Brian divulged that he owed the change to an energy healer. "She transformed my life," he said.

"Really? Hmm. I've had Reiki and it's never done anything for me."

"Oh no," he said, a faraway look settling in his eyes. "This is nothing like Reiki."

Smiling and nodding and thinking he sounded touched, I took the first available exit from the conversation. Following the disastrous appointment with

Adrienne, I flew to my keyboard, hoping he still used the email I had.

"Hi Brian!" I typed, followed by other miscellaneous greetings and salutations. "I was wondering, do you have contact details for that energy practitioner you mentioned?"

Within minutes he sent the name of his healer, Cheryl, who was nearly as speedy. She lived in New Jersey, and even offered to do an impromptu session. Over the phone.

Much as I appreciated her sense of urgency, the phone? How was she supposed to get a read on my energy without seeing me?

My hackles were up, but did I have a choice? I'd been meditating, going to yoga, therapy, meetings. Hell, I even did regular group acupuncture. I booked a compromise with Cheryl—an appointment via Skype.

Cheryl's home office was a plain room without beads or Buddha heads or Om statuary visible. Likewise, her dress was plain—a navy sweatshirt and jeans. The décor was reassuring—Cheryl didn't need the trappings of mysticism to attest to her skills.

She got right to business. "What brings you?"

When I couldn't speak for crying, Cheryl would stop me and ask questions to get back on track. She was oddly interested in my family. Once I gave her the details— mom and dad, still married; one sister, older by two years, never married; and me, the divorced reprobate—I was ready to detail the ex's wrongdoing, but she wanted to talk about my mother.

"You said she has cancer?"

"Yes."

"So she is leaving her body?"

"Well, no, not imminently I don't think."

"Visualize her," she said,

"Uh. That feels a bit off," I said. "I've done a *lot* of work around my family. They weren't excited about being parents, but they did the best they could."

"Family leaves an energetic imprint. This becomes obvious with intimacy issues."

I found this note oddly encouraging. *She can tell I have issues already!*

"Your ego, of course, wants to protect its way of seeing the world. Our work is to cleanse the energy field preventing you from moving on."

No idea what that meant but... okay?

"If you could say anything to her, what would you say to your mother?"

"I'm not sure."

"Yes, you are."

My next words came as a surprise. "Why didn't you ever stand up for me?" I was getting into this.

"Good," she said. "Now, remember a time your mother wasn't there for you. What do you need from her now?"

"A hug?"

"Very good. Picture that hug! Feel it! Let her love envelop you."

Never in a million years would I have anticipated this, but there I was, sitting in my office among my books and candles and Bollywood posters, imagining a hug from my mom.

And it kinda worked.

Following the session with Cheryl the constant thoughts of the ex faded, but I remained subject to weeping. An aspirational bank commercial featuring newlyweds might do it, sending me into the kind of uncontrollable lament I knew my neighbors heard.

Worse yet, I'd lost the ability to meditate, either alone or in the two groups I often joined. Soon as the silence began, my thoughts raced, my body temperature rose, and I'd be unable to sit still. Doubling up on meditation was what saved me when I couldn't get to a psychiatrist before. If that option was no longer available, I feared I'd never stop feeling like hell.

Oblivious as I was to the ways in which I weaponized my practice, four more years would pass before Brown University would release their study, *The Varieties of Contemplative Experience* (a nod to William James' *The Varieties of Religious Experience*, ironically, a text often cited in recovery communities). Essentially a catalog of vipassana meditation's known adverse effects—including fear, anxiety, panic, and paranoia—I was operating under the assumption that vipassana inspired only bliss. Yet I was experiencing such feelings on a regular basis.

Though it's still difficult to find anything contra-dicting the notion that meditation can lead to anything but euphoria, public discourse around trauma and toxic positivity has led to far more widespread understanding.

Another factor contributing to my general mental state was prolonged grief. Though now classified in the DSM-5 as a disorder, at the time I'd never heard of the condition, let alone suspected there was an explanation for my persistent bereavement. With the information at my disposal, I once more became overwhelmed with worry that something was very wrong with me.

"The answer is always more spirituality."

"Maybe I should try ayahuasca," I said to Willy one afternoon, staring not at him but his mixing board in the other room.

Willy stopped work on the suitcase he'd been filling with a drill sergeant's precision atop his kitchen table—he was heading to Germany to meet up with an old flame—and stared in disbelief. "Are you joking?"

"What do you mean?" I asked, pretty sure I knew what he meant. Intended to spur visions of God, ayahuasca is a Mayan drug. Until recently, I would've also dismissed its use as an excuse to get high. But what if this was what I needed?

"It's supposed to be a spiritual magic bullet."

He resumed packing, but with more force. "You know that ain't sober."

"Isn't it? People vomit into buckets all night. They say they don't crave it."

Willy folded his bag. "But they keep going back for more." It wasn't a question.

"It's a religious ritual."

Now Willy laughed. "I missed you converting to Mayan whatever. Come on. You think a drug is going to fix you? That's your addiction talking. There is no magic bullet. You're doing fine."

Except for the part about me doing fine, his logic shattered my fantasy. But I was twitching for *something*.

The money biking saved me on transit enabled me to justify studying yoga at Jivamukti in Union Square. Between the café, bookstore, and scads of programming, I loved the place. Were it not for their strict veganism—a stance I admired but had no desire to attempt—I might've done their teacher training. Still, the studio was my sanctuary.

All their classes began with a lesson. In the years I practiced there, I heard talks on everything from the Hindu goddess Kali to animal welfare to the proper way to poop (in a squat position). During *savasana*, the supine pose at the end of every class, the teacher might play music, have silence, or put on a dharma talk.

That late June afternoon, as the sweat dried on my body and the smell of a street vendor's chicken skewers permeated the room, the teacher put on Pema Chödrön telling a story about one of her students, Jarvis Masters.

After finding Buddhism in prison, Masters wrote a book called *Finding Freedom*. Chödrön relayed a story from his memoir. As the evening's news unfolded, Masters occasionally looked up at a TV set he couldn't hear. The other incarcerated people down the cell block reported who was onscreen—KKK members, Greenpeace protestors, and U.S. Senators. Masters noted, "They all have the same angry faces."

For the duration of this talk, I lay still. Nonreactive. Without my own storyteller monologuing at me, I felt the peace I craved. What if I listened to spiritual teachings in lieu of a silent practice?

Was I cheating, like I'd done at the vipassana retreat with the snacks and the journal? Or was this just guided meditation? Or both? Very soon, I didn't care. Not long after I began this regimen, my ayahuasca fantasies subsided.

Why not explore other "alternative" therapies?

One healing approach I learned during this time was called EFT, emotional freedom technique, or tapping, literally tapping your fingers on your body at specific points. It didn't do much for me and, according to my research, EFT was also widely dismissed by the medical profession, but it seemed to do wonders for a lot of other people. Did I feel flawed for not finding relief from it? Hell no. But I did feel a little guilt.

"Meditation is hard work," a meditation teacher had once warned. "It's not supposed to feel good."

The idea that pain showed accomplishment was hard to drop, but I'd reached the point where I needed relief from feeling like shit more than I needed to find ways to make myself feel worse.

Anything that helped me to drop my inner critic, no matter how briefly, was worth trying, whether it was mindful eating, aromatherapy, or crystals. These attempts might work anywhere from not at all to temporarily. No matter, I'd just move on to something else. Did that make me a spiritual dilettante? Perhaps. But according to whom? If the result was relief from otherwise unbearable pain, what was the upside in upholding these so-called standards?

Earlier that year I'd picked up a used book at The Strand, *Autobiography of a Yogi*. Now I plucked it from my shelf and began reading Paramahansa Yogananda's memoir. Maybe this infamous guide for living as a yogi would illuminate my next step.

Sprinkled among his many insights was his life story, in particular his life-changing experience at the Kumbh Mela, a spiritual festival in India, where he'd met his guru.

Was a guru what I needed? A single visionary who could diagnose my fatal flaw and prescribe the remedy? A quick search revealed not only that the ancient spiritual festival still took place, but that the next one would take place the following year, not long after the film festival would be wrapping. When my work contract ended, I could head back to India. But should I?

Between the two festivals, I'd be gone at least a year. I'd have to give up my classes. And my Manhattan apartment. Was I nearing the cure, or opting for a geographic remedy?

My childhood had been a series of moves, trading one Rust Belt suburb for another. We might as well have been time-traveling. Each new environment was a fresh threat. The one constant, everywhere, was the kids. Vicious.

Once deemed a loser, there was very little that could be done to improve your station. This was long before geotagging. Or the internet. The only tool I had for investigating territories unknown was the *Encyclopedia Britannica*, but knowing a state's bird did little for my social status. Every year or so I'd be dropped into a new location, defenseless as a sea turtle hatchling scrambling for the water, camouflage my only desire.

One afternoon in third grade, Wilson Elementary, I was trying to hide near a clump of trees at recess so I could survey my lunch. Formerly housed inside my beloved, *Cinderella*-inspired lunch box—a cardboard and vinyl construction that had not withstood the day's stomping it got in the coat closet—I noticed spitballs had infiltrated my bologna sandwich. Across the macadam, a herd of classmates caught my attention. They laughed and talked together so easily. *I'll never fit in like that. Never have friends I've known my whole life.*

Then Tracey—the goddess of third grade—floated past.

As she ignored the smiles and waves of her eager classmates and I returned to plucking spittle-coated paper from my food, it occurred that there were various ways to hide in inhospitable surroundings. Popularity was as good a disguise as any.

Near as I could tell, being popular wasn't about being friendly, or even having friends. Popularity was about looking and acting a certain way, like Tracey, with her matching outfits and perfect hair. Or at least not looking like the kind of kid whose lunch box you'd destroy on a whim.

Since I was already cafeteria poison in Reading, Pennsylvania, I set my sights on whatever town was coming next, determined to climb to safety. Float.

In fifth grade—Bay City, Michigan—bell bottoms and a puka shell necklace made me the kind of kid the other kids saved a seat for at lunchtime. But in sixth grade—Birmingham, Alabama—despite adopting the Pappagallo's uniform, I had such trouble with the southern accent I was moved into what they called "special ed." Worse, when I did decode the language, I shot into so-called "advanced classes." By eighth grade—good old Murrysville—thanks to liberal adoption of Aqua Net and Bonne Bell lip gloss, I made cheerleading.

But I couldn't keep up the charade for long. By ninth grade, I lost my place on the squad. In tenth, I was a teenage runaway. After that, I escaped by being high. I knew how to leave, how to reinvent. Did I know how to stay?

Hadn't the extended social experiment I'd pursued with Ricky been the same technique I'd used as a kid? Observe, imitate, correct, and start over.

"I'm never leaving New York City," I told my mother, shortly before I was to leave for Qatar.

"Are you sure you want to pay to store your crap for a whole year?"

Though Mom had never visited my apartment, she'd seen what I owned on video calls. True, I didn't have antiques or fine furnishings—my life in Manhattan had been built from a single suitcase with splurges limited to yoga and writing classes—but I was determined to break this pattern. The poverty mentality was as good a habit to quit as any—I was ready for abundance.

"It's nothing like rent, and anyway, I'll be living rent-free at a hotel the film festival pays for."

With my explanation, my confidence grew. I convinced myself I was ready to face my demons in Doha.

WHY HAVEN'T YOU ANSWERED MY EMAIL YET?

Doha, Qatar 2012

When I'd first arrived in Qatar, the skyline was a blur of cranes and scaffolding, scarcely an impression of what was to come. On my return six years later, though the landscape had not filled in entirely, the visual changes were stark. The change that affected me most however, was the difference in the talent pool.

During my first stint, in addition to difficulty recruiting teammates, I had a hard time sourcing outside support. Our first brochure necessitated bringing in a designer from London, a photographer from Bahrain, and models from the United Arab Emirates. This time around, I put together an in-house team in mere weeks. And they already lived in Doha. But best of all, we put together a group of young Qatari ambassadors to act as the public face of the festival.

Our office was housed in the brand new, I.M. Pei-designed Museum of Islamic Art; my desk faced the emerald jewel that was the Bay of Doha. The setting would've been perfect, but for one thing—the open space floor plan. No doors. No cubicles. Not even partitions. Just an enormous room full of desks. I am just misophonic enough to find working in a noisy environment impossible.

The other major difference was the workload. While I didn't find the duties nearly as challenging, my superiors felt otherwise. I'll never forget leaving an all-staff meeting, only to be confronted by my boss. "Why haven't you answered my email yet?"

I looked down at my Blackberry. She'd sent her missive during the meeting. I was affronted and relieved at once. *If that gathering didn't require each of us paying attention to the goings on, why in hell were we both there?* I thought at her vigorously.

What I said was, "I'll get back to you straightaway." I could only hope her email wasn't a question about whatever had just transpired in the meeting, because there was a third new and different factor at play. For much of that meeting, I'd been present in body alone. I'd begun losing time.

Though I don't recall what set off that particular flight of my imagination, it could have been almost anything. Qatar was one trigger after the next.

For all the enhancements, Doha remained a small

town. Smaller still for a single woman without children. There were only so many places I felt welcome—malls, salons, and five-star hotels. Though I didn't find leisure in shopping and had zero time for massages, I still had to eat. I often gathered over meals with the same people in the same places I had with the ex. Even the newer locations could be an upending.

One place that had not existed when I lived there the first time was the sleek and modern W Hotel where the festival put us up. Sadly, its novelty was not enough to overcome the zealous remembrancer living in my brain.

Throughout my travels in the Arab world, I'd found the five-star hotel experience to typically mean futzy and overdressed—gilt embellishments, curlicues, and loads of wasted space. From the moment I entered the W's muted lobby, I was reminded of the only other such place I'd seen like it during my previous tenure, The Chedi in Oman.

I'd first learned of the hotel on the short flight to Muscat from a colleague extolling its virtues. "The wife and I loved it there," he said, tucking into his Qatar Airways omelet. "When the place first opened, the locals thought the hotel wasn't finished. That's how clean and modern the lines are. Just spectacular." *Maybe I should book a trip to surprise my husband for his birthday*, I thought, so I'd asked for more travel tips. At least that's what I thought we were talking about. When he grabbed my ass in the hotel later that afternoon then sheepishly shrugged off the move, I wasn't so sure anymore.

The incident was so distressing I'd left Oman on the next plane out, questioning whether to tell my spouse. We all worked at Education City—to my horror my partner had taken a job there instead of at Al Jazeera—and I worried that if he knew about the sexual assault it would make for some awkward team meetings. After wrestling all night over what to do, I finally confessed. My ex's response?

"Can you blame him?"

Had he thought I should be flattered? Had he thought about me even then?

Did he think it was *terrific* I was writing a book, or was he that confident it would never come out?

Terrific. The same goddamn word Keith had used.

Fuck me. Adrienne had spotted it right away. I did have a pattern. The same one I'd had with my mom. If I got a whiff of ambivalence in a potential mate, I would change who I was to suit them. Even as a child, I'd never believed in psychics.

"Are you meditating?" Willy asked over WhatsApp after listening to this tale relived.

I stared out my hotel's window at the Arabian Sea, beautiful as it was inaccessible. "Believe it or not, I am chanting."

Though not my favorite practice, it turned out that an SGI Buddhist—Willy's tradition—worked in my office.

"We should chant the lotus sutra," she'd said after I asked about the bag of prayer beads I'd spotted on her desk.

"Sure," I'd agreed, unenthusiastic but willing. Unlike me, by all appearances Gisele was handling the stress of our work environment well—no dark circles under her icy blue eyes, her long brown hair had nary a split end, and there was a calm about her.

Meanwhile, I'd begun to worry I might be sliding toward using drugs and alcohol. Obsessive-compulsive thinking, where I "lost time," had preceded my previous relapse. I'd do anything to avoid that.

In the interest of maintaining my sobriety, I sorted anything non-film-festival-related into one of two categories—either it moved me closer to or further away from a slip. Talking to Willy and chanting were two activities that belonged in the "further away from" column, though, at most, Gisele and I gathered once a month over the course of our five-month assignment.

Just as the end came into view, the Minister of Culture told us we'd have to censor the films.

"Can you spin this as cultural sensitivity?" I was asked.

Mercifully, I was spared this task by the festival's film directors threatening to pull out. Our benefactor, Sheikha Mayassa—the ruler's daughter who lived well in New York but wore the plainest of black wraps when in Qatar—was forced to go up against the Ministry. With less than two weeks to spare, she prevailed—we would screen the films as cut.

Impressed as I was, our Qatari spokespeople were horrified. Every last one of them quit, unwilling to be associated with such scandalous films. Considering that the average episode of *Californication*—screening weekly on Qatar's HBO station—was at least as sexy as our films, I did not see that coming.

"All those sponsees of yours," Willy said in another Skype, reminding me of another milestone unlocked, that at last I'd been asked to mentor others in recovery, "they've been making you ready for this level of clusterfuck."

He had a point, but I didn't see the personal accomplishment. I'd learned far more from working with others than I ever taught, and we only got through the event thanks to my supremely talented in-house Arabic speakers. Meanwhile, another staggering blind spot of mine had been revealed.

A new idea took root. If I was ready to hear Adrienne's wisdom, maybe I should try another vipassana. Though I'd found the retreat curative initially, between my subsequent romantic, work, and familial mishaps, I knew now my work was far from over.

Though I only ever cheated to maintain my sanity, I'd often suspected my contraband—the pen and paper and snacking—had blocked my metamorphosis. What if I returned and took the plunge without a net? No writing implements or food. Just me and my thoughts. Would that make a difference? And would that difference be for the good?

There was one way to find out.

FIREWORKS!

Goa, 2012-2013

My first stop in India was to drop my bags in Goa.

I'd reached out to Jenny about my impending stay—not-so-secretly hoping she'd ask me to work for her again, even if it was in her shop—but instead she hooked me up with a sweet room for the season.

"The couple who was living there is leaving," she'd emailed. "Two of my students are there now, and I'm sure I can help you find a new roommate when they leave. The place is huge and cheap as chips."

She wasn't kidding. By renting for the season, my room came out to about $70 a month. Better yet, I had a home base. One less thing to dither over while I chased nirvana through my fault-finding tour.

Thus I'd come to be in Goa for New Year's Eve as the countdown started rolling, staring at the man I'd dubbed, Yogi Bear. He was on the beach, making out. With

181

someone else.

"Three!"

Had I really considered going to the Persian Gulf with that guy?

I looked around the party—the fairy lights, the waves, and my friends in the sand—all of it was exactly the same as it had been the moment before. The judge and jury were in my head. Allowing YB's choice to mean anything about me would've been my choice. *I can still enjoy the night*, I thought, blinking back tears from the corners of my eyes.

The countdown to midnight raged on.

"Two!"

"Excuse me."

I turned to find one of the young men I'd met over dinner earlier that night. My breath caught in my throat.

The dinner group had included Annie, one of Jenny's yoga instructors, and her boyfriend Ben, who was also staying for the season. His friends from "uni"—in town for the holidays—were also seated at the table.

As part of a ruse I was now questioning, YB and I had downplayed our budding relationship among the yoga community, many of whom I'd known since my previous stay. We'd arrived at the restaurant separately, and proceeded to sit at opposite ends of the table. I didn't know who was at the other end of the table, but my end was so good-looking and funny, I worried YB might think I was losing interest. I attempted some sexy texts.

`I am so ready to eat.`

Separate text.

`You!`

Maybe that was what killed it.

Anyway, now standing before me was one of Ben's friends, the one I'd dubbed Taller, Darker, and Handsomer.

"I hope you don't mind," said TD&H in his gorgeous Aussie accent.

"But I think you're right sexy, and I'd like to kiss you."

"One!"

The crowd roared as I went from utter dejection to acceptance to wonder. Now I, too, was making out on the beach. When the cheering ended, so did our kiss. But TD&H wasn't finished with me yet.

"I don't mean to sound too forward," he said, looking me right in the eye. "But I'd like to take you home."

Overhead, a fireworks show began. Happy New Year to me.

A wide smile spread across my face that I quickly covered. TD&H was being serious. *This kid from uni has no idea how old I am.*

Since discovering how my ex had swapped me for a different model, my desire to replace him had been rekindled. I reckoned my dating exploits were a diversion that had to stop. TD&H would provide that rush of gratification, but then our interlude would pass and nothing would have changed. I wanted something more fulfilling, more lasting.

I patted TD&H on the chest. "You're sweet," *whatever your name is*, "but I should be getting on."

As I wound my way out of the party, I stopped to say goodbye to my friends. For some reason—bragging?—

when I got to Annie and Ben, I had to spill.

"You won't believe this, but your friend over there?" I said, motioning to TD&H.

"Rob?" Ben asked.

"Is it Rob?" I laughed. "Anyway, he just tried to pick me up!"

To Ben this was no laughing matter. "What? You're never gonna meet a better looking Australian. Go back and git 'im."

Ben's urging flipped a switch.

Though YB's deceit had briefly reignited my concern about my inability to see plain truths—as I'd feared in Qatar—in that moment another truth was clear. My response had inclined toward self-preservation. I'd never find a world without suffering, but my traumatized self didn't need to prevail. I could be my own safe space. Exercise my agency as I saw fit. *Nam myoho renge kyo.*

Later that night, after enjoying Rob up close, I had to ask. "How *do* you keep your body in this shape*?*"

"Cricket," he answered, puffing his chest.

Wasn't cricket a game that involved lots of standing around and tea breaks? How could that level of fitness possibly result?

Right. He was all of twenty. Besides, the time for talking was over. No need to pretend. Though Rob's midnight appearance was a testament to the emotional turn my feelings had taken, he wasn't integral to the process.

"Let's go back to the party!"

Soon I was on the dance floor with another someone, having a blast. I didn't notice if YB was still around. But I did bump into Ben, who gave me a huge grin.

"You're back? You're a legend!"

For the first time in a long time, I felt like one.

Even if it was this mood that queered the vipassana, I'm eternally grateful for both.

THE AFTERNOON
SESSION IS IN PROGRESS

Karnataka, 2013

A few days into the New Year, I was on the road to
Bengaluru. After leaving behind the dirt roads, instead of
sparking concern that I was in the wrong place, this time I
knew the barrenness meant we were getting closer.

"Old student?" the person at check-in asked. Anyone
who'd done a vipassana before was called "old," still I
winced, feeling ancient at forty-five. Yet if I hadn't been
before, I don't know that I would've been willing to try
this. One of the benefits of being an "old" student was
that I could join a sit for a mere three days, not enough
time to really lose my mind.

And I can still leave at any time, I promised myself.

When she handed me the list of rules I didn't hesitate.
Happily, I wasn't asked to fill out the form again—I still

hadn't mentioned my mental health history. At least I didn't have to actively lie.

After taking my cell phone, the attendant motioned toward the space beyond. "Once you've found a cot," she said. "The afternoon session is in progress. You may take any available cushion."

I didn't need more tour than that to know what to do next, until—as I headed for the women's dorm to deposit my tote—I caught sight of the new meditation hall. A long white building fronted by a pillared porch and topped with a coral-colored tile roof, I couldn't wait to see the inside.

In the sleeping quarters I nabbed the first open cot, slid my bag under the bedside table (that was new), and headed toward the shed, which was now a bona fide hall. With a veranda.

Appreciating the overhang's shade from the midday sun, I slipped off my flip-flops and went inside. The room gleamed. Its polished concrete floor was lined with cushions, men on one side, women on the other. Grabbing a few extra pillows on the way in, I took the first available spot on the women's side and got down to business—reviewing my life in order to suss out my character defects.

Something Willy often said was: "You can't know what you don't know." What struck me now, from my vipassana perch, was something I hadn't known until I sat to begin my contemplation—I didn't have all that much to mull over.

The festival had provided enough of a financial cushion that I'd be able to stay in India for the duration of my six-month visa. I'd largely written my book and my agent was shopping it. Home, I knew, was New York City. And, while I still hadn't figured out my fatal flaw, my love life felt less catastrophic. After the New Year's Eve party, I'd come around to embracing my friend Ophira's advice, "Men are like buses. Miss one and, sooner or later, another will come along."

Though I have no notes from the sit itself, three things stood out: One, I could feel my breath (undoubtedly the active smoking I'd been doing prior to arriving in India had played a role in my earlier difficulties). Secondly, I'd developed a seat I could maintain without having to run from the room constantly. So third, I wasn't aggravated by Goenka's instructions. I was able to listen, finding it much like the guided meditations I'd been doing back in Manhattan. One such teaching still stands out.

"You observe the gross physical form—blond hair, brunette hair, dark hair—so beautiful. Now that hair has come in your soup." Goenka laughed. "This is disgusting. Take it away! What happened to the beauty?"

When I heard this story at the ashram, I had the sort of insight that held me in bliss-seeking fantasy. When I thought about my judgmental ways, I recognized how terrible it felt to judge. An internalized belief emerged— feeling bad was the punishment I deserved for being critical in the first place. A worthy discovery, though one I'm sure—had I brought this revelation into therapy— Adrienne would've suggested contradicting. "Is that true? How does it serve you?" The trap was looking, the constant, microscopic inspection for misdeeds, a search that worked best at keeping my anguish alive.

When the bell rang at the end of the first sit, I could stand without the acrobatics. As I nonetheless limped out, a surprising thought crossed my mind.

I don't hate myself enough to do this.

I didn't?

In my vipassana-slowed brain, I toyed with this thought. Was I doing something I'd already done and expecting different results?

My first sponsor, Ruth, came to mind, packing her Pall Malls on the table between us. "When you don't know what to do," tap, tap, tap, "don't do anything." Tap, tap.

In this case, doing nothing meant staying where I was. Or did it?

As I collected my toothbrush and toothpaste from the dorm, my sluggish brain pondered the question. While brushing at the long sink fronting the women's toilet, I reasoned it only made sense to stay through the afternoon refreshment I knew they'd be serving—bhel puri, a savory puffed rice tossed with tamarind, peanuts, and coriander.

Later, as I crunched away, a delicious note of coriander hit my mouth. *Why not stay?* That future miracle I longed for—a final shedding of my intimacy-repelling quality or qualities—was more likely to come about if I knew to whom I should address my requests. The same was true if I intended to stay sober for the long haul.

One of the main tenets of 12-Step recovery is that

sobriety is achieved through spiritual means. When I first grasped this methodology, my only experience with anything god-like had been through the Catholic church.

There I'd learned I could only address The One God through a priest who then spoke—on my behalf—to Jesus, himself a stand-in for the big guy. These chats consisted of me apologizing for failing to meet unattainable expectations. Where was the part where I got something? Oh yeah, after death. No thanks. Then there was the fact that the church didn't have female clergy, only nuns who had to marry Jesus. Another no, thank you.

Then there was my mom's Catholicism. Though I never asked why, Mom never took communion at church. I suspected her punishment was handed down by whatever priest she'd first told about being pregnant "out of wedlock." That guy had undoubtedly forgotten the penance my mother couldn't relinquish. A hearty, *fuck that*.

Fortunately, 12-Step recovery stopped short of dictating a supreme being, instead relying on the unfortunate moniker, the Higher Power. Such latitude was how I'd been able to maintain any kind of membership. Lacking any better idea, I'd glommed onto my boyfriend's god concept.

"Truth isn't fair," Jeffrey was fond of saying. "That's why it's the only Higher Power I can imagine in a world where bad things happen."

Jeffrey's Truth had been enough until, in the wake of his death, it offered only the coldest of comforts. Yet somehow after nearly twenty-five years in and around recovery, my definition of a divinity and its powers remained murky. After all I'd been through, why not devise a Higher Power with more possibility?

I would stay.

Before the evening sit began, a group of us waited on the cafeteria's steps. Palm and mimosa trees had been planted around the edges, not quite the verdant wonders I'd seen online when first researching vipassanas, but a damn sight more inviting than the square of scorched earth that had greeted me before.

When the robed man (a different robed man, though he still sat near the boombox) appeared in my periphery, one of the women rose to pull him aside. On my first sit, I'd have been livid—*She's* speaking*! How dare she?* But I'd discovered that spoken interactions were routine. The reason their exchange stood out, however, is because of the words I heard him speak.

"There is no knee apart from the mind, sister," he said, his voice as gentle as a baby's blanket. "But please, sit in a chair until the sitting is more comfortable."

Like the hair in the soup, experience was about context. Where once I might've heard his words as an invitation to suffer, as in, "You're not fooling yourself with that quick fix for your pain." I now heard the compassion. "More suffering is not the answer to suffering." It was a refreshing middle ground between my family's gym-centric "no pain, no gain" ethos and my fear of surrender.

The following morning during our silent sit—not even the tape played during the first sit of the day—my head bobbed. Automatically, I reached up to fluff my bangs onto my face. *Classic Steph.*

My best friend in high school, Steph, had shown me how to brush my hair forward so I could nap in class undetected. Despite a daily regimen of Black Beauties, as we called speed, I needed the sleep. That was when the other kids started calling me alkie.

Straightening my spine, I urged myself to refocus on my Higher Power; pains rippled through my lower half. I didn't react. I'd noticed pain without moving before, but this was different, a blank, unselfconscious stillness accompanying the moment. Once I noticed the sensation it was over, but I was delighted.

Since the first vipassana I'd often recalled Goenka's teaching that our thought habits could be fleeting (like ripples in water), more marked (like lines drawn on a sandy beach), or etched (like grooves cut into rock). According to Goenka, practice could dissolve any level of imprint. For so long I'd felt trapped in my habitual responses, but that moment of stillness signaled something fresh.

Shortly before heading to Qatar, I'd read a book about the brain's potential to heal and change, *My Stroke of Insight* by Dr. Jill Bolte Taylor. A brain researcher, Dr. Taylor had—in the midst of having a stroke—chronicled her experience and the ensuing research. I was all in until she suggested the life span of an emotion was about ninety seconds. Of course I agreed with her basic premise, that thoughts kept experiences alive. But emotions? I should've gotten past Jeffrey's death in a minute and a half? And what did that say about the yearslong process I was yet in the midst of? *Nothing,* I'd decided, unwilling to make myself wrong.

Though I disagreed with the author's emotional lifespan estimate, I'd discovered the fraction of time I had available to redirect before responding out of habit. My tragical thinking was softening at last.

The vipassana ended.

Proud I'd withstood the rigors again, this finale wasn't accompanied by the same sense of triumph as before. My chief recognition was the unlikelihood I'd ever return. In the past, I'd have seen this as a failure, but I felt no such sense of self-recrimination. Though I didn't yet appreciate it, learning to meet life from a place of worthiness was the journey. I still thought of my quest— which had begun in dramatic fashion by rendering me smoke-free—as a portal to my salvation. But what if I didn't need to be redeemed?

FLEXING THE MUSCLE OF LOVE

Goa, 2013

Goa is overrun with breathtaking scenery. My chief memories of the southern Indian state—the ones that don't involve active questing—consist of riding my Honda Aviator scooter through twisting ribbons of road while listening to The National, Stars, or Thievery Corporation. Unlike my typical goal-oriented self, when traversing these less touristic paths I made unplanned stops to snap photos of palm-filled valleys and oceanside sunsets, grab a drink from roadside chai wallahs, or take meals at village cafés.

I often wondered about the mansions I spied along these roads, nestled amidst lush vegetation. The homes mixed Dravidian pillars with geometric Islamic tiles and Portuguese terracotta roofs. To my delight, the place

Jenny had hooked me up with was one such structure where I had the entire second floor to myself (essentially a single room), complete with a Juliette balcony.

From my second story perch, I could see Jenny's shala, making this the ideal spot to finish writing my Qatar book and not become a recluse. First I typed up everything I could remember about the vipassana.

Goenka's message was the same—the instructions were taped after all. Whether I heard him differently or missed his words during my many bathroom breaks, much of what I heard struck me as new information. Like Goenka's insistence that the Buddha, through sitting still, had become aware of molecules moving inside his body.

Inasmuch as I recalled Goenka's words, I typed: "The Buddha found that the entire material universe was made up of particles he called kalāpas. They are not solid, only vibration. This constant stream of waves or particles that we think of as self is constantly moving. It is an illusion."

I stopped typing to consider. "Was this stream what I'd perceived when I had a nervous breakdown all those years ago?" I finally wrote. *Are drugs the gateway?* I wondered, but didn't commit to the page. The last thing I needed to add to this mix was some idealized drug fantasy. Regardless of the story's plausibility, vipassana practitioners weren't expected to perceive subatomic movement. Breath on the lip sufficed.

One sense that had never left me since that break with reality, however, was the illusion of the self as separate. Thinking now about that vacuum tube of light, the energy that made up all things I typed, "Self is an illusion."

There's that psychedelic rock wisdom again, I

thought.

"Are all philosophies the same in the end?" I wrote. But I had no wish to sink into despair. I wanted to work with the thoughts trying to emerge, so I stopped and took a few breaths.

Whether Buddha discovered subatomic movement or not, it was real and continually taking place. Unlike a bearded man in the sky, molecular vibration was something I'd learned about in a science class. The ghost in the body's machine. Energy.

"Energy is always felt within," I typed. "The sensation can be good or bad, and can affect other people. Could energy be my Higher Power?"

The afterlife was an aspect of religions I found absurd, but there was no denying our component parts recycled after death. Energy didn't just disappear.

"Energy is, was, and always will be." I typed, my Inner Catholic rearing its way out. "It's indestructible.

"Since our energy exists apart from our physical form, that implies a moral imperative."

Truth never had, I thought, remembering Jeffrey's words about his impartial benefactor. Not only was Truth a steely manager, as I'd discovered after Jeffrey's death, it could have a problematic, malleable quality.

Cultivating positive energy—not the same thing as positivity—made sense. More often than not, I could conjure positive energy by tuning into my surroundings.

The next morning after yoga, a group of us from Jenny's shala went for breakfast to Baba au Rhum, a lovely house cum restaurant run by French expats. That morning on the restaurant's open-air patio, surrounded by dense vegetation, instead of eating my almond croissant, I found myself gazing at Annie.

Annie had been one of the teachers at my yoga training five years earlier. She and her partner back in Australia quarreled and broke up so often long-distance, I was sure their relationship wouldn't survive the season. Their struggle was classic: she wanted more commitment than he wanted to give. Now here she was, with him, in Goa, eating breakfast.

By what alchemy? I wondered. And, *Should they be together at all?*

"What're you looking at?" Annie asked, which sounded much friendlier in her Australian tones but was still a difficult question.

"Uhh," I began, aware my thoughts were inappropriate. My romantic life left no room for judging.

"Don't be a cunt, Annie," chimed in our friend, Nathan, using his favorite word, which also sounded better in his British accent. "She's obviously still a bloody mess. Now, Lisa. Tell me. What *is* wrong with you?"

I loved these people so much.

"I'm definitely spacey after a vipassana." I nodded, wanting to go somewhere with the conversation I'd been having in my head. "But I was thinking. About love. The nature of love. What is it even?"

"Oh my God, I may need to start day-drinking. Garçon!" Nathan squealed, snapping his fingers in a campy search for a waiter. Not that there were waiters, or alcohol at this breakfast establishment, though the people at the next table over were smoking a giant spliff.

We all laughed, but I really wanted to know what they thought.

"Hear me out," I said when the laughter subsided. "We have this one word when there are so many kinds of love. There's love of things, then there's love of beings. I can love ice cream, and I can love you. But as a society, we have this idea that romantic love is the ideal kind. And the longer, the more monogamous the relationship, the better."

"It's not better, it's just easier to be with one person," Annie said. "But I think the feeling's the same."

"Ben must be quite the stud," Nathan said. "I've had way better sex with one-night stands. Would you consider lending him out?"

"Lisa said love, not sex," Annie protested.

"So he's not any good in bed?"

"Nathan!"

"Answer the question!" Nathan winked.

"Guys!" I interrupted. "This is what I mean. One word, totally different connotations. Or are they? Like, I am *loving* this croissant. And right now, that feels about as valid as any love I could feel. Does it matter who or what the love is for? Or is feeling love the ultimate goal, whatever the form?"

"Different isn't better," Annie said. "Just different. Though sometimes different is terrible."

"Ben, don't believe a word she says!" Nathan said, leaning closer to Ben. "Nobody ever says that about *me*."

"As long as you're flexing the muscle of love," Annie said. "It's a good thing."

"I'd like to see everyone flexing their love muscles," Nathan cried.

After that, there was no getting back to anything approaching my level of earnest. But when I returned to my balcony later that afternoon, I went at the topic in my journal.

"Maybe the Higher Power energy I need to concentrate on is love," I typed.

I sat back, barely rereading that sentence before doubt peeked its way through. My mind created a poster: The words GOD IS LOVE juxtaposed over the image of a kitten. *Gods, no.*

Returning to my laptop, I felt for another angle. Willing as I was to entertain mystical ideas, I wanted to avoid the causal connections emblematic of magical thinking.

Looking across the courtyard toward Jenny's shala, I recalled a talk I'd heard back at Jivamukti. In it Ram Dass, the iconic psychologist who'd eschewed Western life then gone on to write 1971's best-selling *Be Here Now*, told a story about his teacher.

After letting a resentment with another student build, Ram Dass took his complaint to his master. "Tell the truth," his guru advised.

Soon enough, Ram Dass was back. Telling the truth hadn't gone well.

This time his guide said, "Love everyone."

Frustrated, Ram Dass replied, "The truth is, I don't love everyone."

His teacher laughed. "Stop lying to yourself."

When I first heard the story it made no sense. I related to Ram Dass. Now, my irrationality was clear. If I accepted myself and others as they were—the good, the bad, the ugly—my fear told me I was condoning. Such acceptance would allow the "bad" to fester and grow. Not loving everyone was another strategy, a way to hold myself—and everyone else—accountable.

From my second story perch, I looked back toward Jenny's shala, noticing how the leaves blocked the sun. The resulting shadow print shifted with each breeze, gently but undeniably altering everything it touched. Surfaces, I was reminded, were not what they seemed.

An ancient proverb came to mind: "No man steps into the same river twice, for he is not the same man, and it is not the same river."

Nowhere did this feel more true than in my family. Though Mom and I spoke daily, after she'd declared herself free of cancer my visits had returned to a holiday occasion schedule. Yet before leaving the States, I'd gone to visit my parents in Murrysville. While I was aware that Dad had developed a special diet for Mom, something based on her blood type and brimming with antioxidants, I was shocked to see the change in action.

The first morning I awoke, surprised to hear the sounds of a blender whirring in the kitchen, drawers opening and closing, and the strike of a knife against a cutting board. Blurry-eyed, I halted at the far end of the room, stopped by what I saw. And smelled. In all the time I'd known him, my father couldn't find a spoon in his own kitchen. Yet there he was, crafting a malodorous brew of canned peaches, cottage cheese, and cod liver oil. My coffee would have to wait.

I joined my mother on the family room couch, a U-shaped sectional that hadn't been replaced since they'd bought the house thirty years earlier.

"Is he making that for your benefit or mine?"

Mom shook her head. "Nope. He makes them every day."

Before I could say more, Dad appeared, drink in hand. I reached for the glass to cut short his journey around the seating area, but he yanked his arm away and stomped the whole way around to hand Mom her glass himself.

Mom struggled to take a swallow. "Thanks, hon."

"That is rank!" I said, as soon as Dad had left for work.

"It tastes like a mistake," Mom said, forcing down another gulp.

"Why do you drink it?"

She shrugged. "Can't hurt."

"What about when you're on chemo? Isn't it hard to eat at all then?"

"The treatment's really advanced, hon," she said.

I smelled an untruth in her repeating that line but didn't say anything.

Thinking back on our exchange now, I marveled at my parents' love and how it had changed over the years. Their bond had always been evident; I'd been the one who didn't see. Looking into the yard, I saw love was everywhere: in the green leaves poking through cracks in the sidewalk, a three-legged dog scratching his back in the dirt, the way my father attended to my mother. The optimism was heartbreaking.

Certainly, love was something to worship.

A deep feeling of contentment overtook me. Love was bigger and more sparkly than truth or energy, and with just the slightest bit of focus, I could always access something to love. No need to wait, love was only ever as far away as finding something to admire.

Satisfied, I snapped my laptop shut. I was ready to meet my guru. Soon as I bought some sweaters. The Maha Kumbh Mela—where I was heading next—took place in the northern Indian state of Uttar Pradesh where it could be quite cold in the winter.

I thought I was so prepared.

AIRDASH

Uttar Pradesh, 2013

"Tutah putah, but what else is it not?" I overheard a tall, distinguished-looking woman saying at the Varanasi airport. Her Hinglish, a spoken mishmash of Hindi and English, signaled that she was part of India's burgeoning upper-class society, people comfortable blending modernity with tradition.

She waved at the general disorder in the baggage claim area, where there were no visible lines, just people and suitcases flung about at odd angles, but it was clear she was speaking to the two women toting Gucci handbags to match their salwar kameez, long colorful Indian print tunics and wide-legged pants. I tried not to stare as I strained to listen, and anyway her patois ensured that most of us—myself included—wouldn't be able to understand the conversation. I didn't mind. I loved listening in to pick up whatever mashups I could, like "airdash," meaning hurry. Then, like a life raft thrown my way, I distinctly heard her say "Kumbh Mela."

Despite active Googling, I hadn't found any sort of guide to the Kumbh. Not even a tour bus. The only accommodation I found was in a tent—no toilet—for $440 a night. With a five-night minimum. Had I been able to shell out that astronomical sum, the tent wasn't even on Kumbh grounds. The last thing this journey needed was the added challenge of a daily trek.

The Kumbh Mela has been called the largest human gathering on the planet, visible in satellite images. This year's spiritual festival would be a Maha, or Grand Kumbh Mela. The Maha Kumbh was expected to attract some one hundred million people during its month and a half long run. To put that in perspective, Times Square gets around thirty-nine point two million visitors per year.

Thus I'd decided to get as close to the Kumbh as possible and sort my festival plan on the ground, which was how I'd come to be at the Varanasi airport, eavesdropping in baggage claim.

Varanasi is India's holiest city, considered the ideal spot to be cremated before being sent to the next world via the Ganges. Surely, I'd locate fellow travelers coming or going from the Kumbh. I'd borrow their itineraries. Not that I imagined this search would be quick. A fan of creature comforts like running water and electricity, I was hoping to find someone without a backpack. These Gucci-clad women might be an overcorrection, but I had to start somewhere.

"Excuse me. Did I just hear you mention the Kumbh Mela?" I asked disingenuously. "Are you heading there?"

"Why yes," the tall woman said. "It's a Maha Kumbh. This kind of opportunity only comes along once in a lifetime!"

Score. "I'm heading there myself. Do you know of any places to stay?"

The women exchanged glances; the tall one spoke again. "You are going to the Kumbh and you have no accommodation?"

"But everything is booked," interjected her shorter, more matronly companion.

"Tsk tsk. No. The Mauni is finishing," their third companion said.

I couldn't be sure, but I assumed she was referring to the festival's most auspicious bathing day. One of the Kumbh's main attractions was taking a dip in the Ganges in order to absolve sins and/or cure bodily ailments. More interested in the guru search, I'd timed my trip to avoid those even bigger crowds.

"Are you heading there now?" I asked, anticipating they might be able to offer me news from the scene.

"Achha, no! We are spending the weekend in Varanasi," the tall woman said.

This was getting better all the time. I was heading to Varanasi.

"Leave it with me," she went on. "My name is Preeti. This is Padma and Ashima. We are going to meet with our pandit, but here is my mobile. Please, call me tomorrow."

Before leaving Manhattan, I'd pre-booked my hotel in

Varanasi's Old City, a place I'd read about in Geoff Dyer's *Jeff in Venice, Death in Varanasi*. The book, a fictional tale of a man who leaves behind his self-indulgence for absolution and becomes a monk, didn't leave me with the desire to become a monk, though it had sparked interest in this section of the city, an ancient stone warren bursting with shops, tea houses, and small hotels and directly abutting the Ganges.

Varanasi itself was widely known for its absolution services. Hindus believed that cremation along its shores could free the newly deceased from the cycle of reincarnation. Though I'd booked the weekend prepared to spend the entire time searching for Kumbh lodging, now I was free to roam the city. That my freedom would be curtailed by the city itself only hit me after my airport taxi dropped me off at the Old City's stone archway.

"It is there," he said, shaking his head. "But no cars."

Once I'd alit from his car and wheeled my suitcase to the portal, I saw why. The cramped alley inside teemed with people and cows and scooters rampaging through what appeared to be a maze at astonishing speeds. Was there enough room for me?

My eyes flew from the doorways to the curbs to the street corners to my phone. I had an address, but I didn't see any house numbers. Or street names for that matter. If I did wander in, how would I find my hotel?

A motorcyclist brushed up next to me. "Ride, miss?"

Though the vehicle seemed impossibly large for the space, my only alternative would've been to take on the labyrinth alone, with my rolling suitcase. I hopped on. By the third time my guide stopped for directions I made up my mind to jump off the next time we stopped. Luckily, our next stop was in front of my hotel.

Time to explore.

After checking in, I went straight to the riverbank walkway behind the hotel. The wide quay featured more offerings than I could absorb, and I didn't have to worry about getting lost—it was a straight shot. Yet as I strolled the wide sidewalk—alive with ancient temples and palaces, wide, steep stairwells, and restaurants—the sense of craving was overwhelming. The path brimmed with beggars and pilgrims and priests, all of us wanting something. When I heard an offer, I practically leapt.

"Ganga aarti by boat. Sunset boat ride!"

Before my arrival I'd read about these boat tours without developing any interest. The idea of gliding along the river to gape as families sent their loved ones to the next life felt intrusive. Now on the ground, however, I saw that the cremation ceremonies were celebrations; it was quite an achievement to afford such a sendoff. Besides, there was no avoiding rites that were conducted continuously, every day. Watching from a boat seemed less meddlesome than gaping from directly among the mourners.

Soon our small boat was pushing off amid dozens of other vessels of various shapes and sizes. I thought we'd traverse the riverbank, but instead we motored into a heavily trafficked spot where the guide cut the engine. As the air filled with smoke from the ghats and the skies darkened with clouds of ravenous mosquitoes, neither my long-sleeved knit jacket nor the scarf I held over my face provided defense—those little assholes bit right through.

My bug spray was in my bag back at the hotel; I was trapped for the duration. *I can't think of a goddamn thing to love right now*, I thought, curling into myself and closing my eyes until the cruise finally ended.

When we banked, I clambered to disembark along with the disbursing crowd. I'd barely hit the boardwalk before a young girl tapped at my hip. Her other hand held a flower and candle, cocooned inside a coconut shell. Looking back toward the water, I saw hundreds of such lights, a sea of floating stars.

The hunger of grief, palpable as the smoke in the air, lived in this expanse of longing, each a wish for the future. I bought one to send afloat, but instead of making a wish I sent the shell into the water with a prayer of gratitude, *Thank you for the life that brought me here.*

The thought surprised. Whenever I heard people say they were grateful for their addiction, I recoiled. My gratitude was not for my divorce, or Jeffrey's death, or my addiction, but for many teachers I'd met along the way who'd shown me how to meet life's challenges.

Is this appreciation more powerful than anger?

Only no, power wasn't quite right. Gratitude was more sustainable.

A grateful heart was the best of loving, all outward bound with no sense of need attached to the mood. Even at its best, giving thanks was typically conditional, whereas—even at its worst—gratitude had no victims or perpetrators. With these realizations, a sense of triumph followed me back to my hotel.

But so did those tiny biting assholes.

From the doorway I could see that I'd failed to fully

close the window, allowing in a swarm of mosquitoes. Or were they gnats? No matter, the air was black with their bodies, as were the curtains and bedding. I slammed the door shut and rushed to the lobby.

LOVE. LOVE. LOVE.

"Hi. I know it's late, but is there any chance I can change into another room? My room is infested with bugs!"

"Oh, sorry ma'am," the man behind the desk said, smiling. "We're fully booked."

FUCK! Of course they were fully booked. Thanks to the Kumbh, everything would be. I started digging for my phone—maybe Preeti could help—when the man said, "Why don't you go to our rooftop café for dinner?"

Eat? At a time like this?

"We can clear your room for you. It will be ready after some time."

I could not imagine any time reentry would be possible. If they somehow managed to clear the room, what disgusting chemicals would be left behind? Then again, the inside of anything was preferable to the alleyways outside.

LOVE. LOVE. LOVE.

"Which way is the restaurant?"

The hotel's café overlooked the Old City. Squinting at the dim lights, I imagined the surrounding hills as a bejeweled cape, a thing of beauty to appreciate. Soon enough however, I started listening in on the conversation at the table beside mine.

"I hear this is the worst year yet," a man who sounded British said.

"I would not bathe my dog in that water," agreed his companion, an Indian though I could not tell from where exactly. "The samples I collected today show an abysmal water quality."

"Sewage?" the Brit asked.

"Mmm. And they drink it right from the tap. It's a miracle there's anyone alive to see to the ghats."

Up till that moment, I'd been considering bathing in the Ganges during the Kumbh, alternating between curious and queasy at the idea. Their conversation cinched it. Definitely not.

Returning to my room later, I found the space mosquito-free and without smell or sticky residue of any kind. If I hadn't seen the swirl of insects myself, I would've doubted there'd been any. I had no clue how they'd eradicated the swarm but as I settled into my sheets, I decided I didn't want to know. A stark realization occurred—if I'd been there with a lover, we'd have undoubtedly gotten into a fight about who'd left the window open. For once, I was not simply content to be alone, I was ecstatic.

By the time I reconnected with Preeti, however, I was excited for her company. I couldn't wait to find my divine other half, and she was going to help me.

LOVE. LOVE. LOVE.

THEY MAKE MOVIES
ABOUT IT

Uttar Pradesh, 2013

According to Hindu legend there was once a great fight between gods and demons over an elixir of immortality. During their battle, four drops of the liquid fell to the earth along the Ganges. The Kumbh Mela rotates between these points on a twelve-year cycle, stopping at each spot once every four years when the stars align and the Ganges and Yamuna rivers come into confluence with the mythical (i.e., not physically real) Sarasvati River.

Owing to these astrological shifts, each Kumbh is unique. Massive tent cities are built to accommodate seekers, all constructed solely for the event. Even with the soundest engineering, handling 100 million people is a formidable challenge. The year I visited, forty-two people

211

died when a footbridge near the train station collapsed; the news was everywhere the morning we set out from Varanasi.

Preeti had instructed me to meet up with her car at six in the morning, then follow her, Padma and Ashima to the festival. Gratingly, I wasn't able to get more info from her, like an address or the name of where we'd be staying.

"Have your driver call mine if we're separated." Preeti smiled. "The gods are with us. They both speak Bhojpuri."

Hailing from Mumbai, Preeti spoke a different dialect altogether. I sat back and rolled up the window to keep out the morning chill and smog.

"Would you like AC?" the driver asked.

The gods were with us. I was not expecting this luxury. Though the mornings were quite cold, by the time we reached our destination, Allahabad, I could imagine the inside of the car turning stuffy. And that was when I thought we were a mere three hours away.

As we drew closer to the event, the roads clogged with foot traffic, whole families with carts and animals, our pace slowed to a crawl.

"Getting lost at the Kumbh Mela is so common," Anil turned his head to announce with a grin. "They make movies about it!"

Why is he not looking at the road? I wondered as he swerved to avoid a knot of pedestrians loaded down with suitcases.

"Very famous one, three brothers are lost and raised by totally different families!" He was still facing me and I noticed that Preeti's car was nowhere in sight. "But at the end they are reunited. Very funny!"

Later when I googled I learned that, indeed, the Kumbh was its own Bollywood genre, and even more specifically, lost at the Kumbh. We were lost and we'd not yet made it to the Kumbh.

At last, we crested a mound in the road and a small city, made entirely of tents, appeared. The campground, I'd later read, spanned 4,784 acres. *Where would I even begin to spend a single day in this vast encampment?*

When we snaked our way into the tent city an hour later, I was mesmerized by the crowd—myriad naked men covered in ash, sadhus atop brightly painted wagons draped in marigold phool malas, and circus-like tent entrances outfitted with megaphones, ads and banners but leading to what I did not know. Nothing was written in English. *Where was Preeti?*

Anil drove in circles. Or was it a straight line? Impossible to say.

Looking around the tent city, I realized that just making it here was an accomplishment. But was this a goal I wanted to achieve? I hate crowds and camping. Had my brazen desire to vault past a spiritual plateau been the thing that blinded me? Maybe I should ask the driver to drive me straight back to the Varanasi airport.

Preeti appeared in the driver's window. "There you are!" she effused, as if I'd been off on a sightseeing romp. "Come, come! Hurry! We've got a service to attend."

Dragging my bag in the dirt, I passed through the enormous, pillared archway we'd halted in front of. The canvas entry was emblazoned with bright colors and images. Of a woman, round-faced and sporting saffron.

Among the thousands of tents that made up the Kumbh, had I miraculously landed in my guru's tent?

Beyond the threshold I spied a circle of what I assumed were her followers, clad in all-white robes and seated around a fire in a three-quarter thrust arrangement. Where the stage would've been, a single row of Indian men played traditional instruments: a tabla, sitars, and a harmonium. Other than the band, everybody taking part in the fireside call and response ritual was white.

Despite my best efforts, my spiritual wandering often led me into communities largely comprised of other white people. Part of my desire to attend the Kumbh was the wish that I might discover a spiritual path free of Christian mores. Seeing this assembly of people who looked like me was, to put it mildly, disappointing.

"Come!" Preeti motioned me to follow her. "You must sign in and then we go. The holiest man in all of India is coming."

At the check-in I was given a key for what turned out to be a padlock on my door, though I only used it once; afterward the door remained unlocked. Apparently, I was going to be sharing the room with multiple people who weren't Preeti. Her crew had set up in a separate room across the courtyard. My room was bare but for the cots, so after dropping my suitcase, I returned to the courtyard.

"The car is here," Preeti announced, surprising me from behind as she pointed to a brand new, gleaming white SUV. Clearly this trip was going to be one surprise after the next.

"This is Ramana, he is our pandit," Preeti told me as I climbed into the back, where Padma and Ashima waited.

I pressed my palms together namaste-style and bowed, hoping the greeting was acceptable to whichever tradition of Hinduism he represented. Hindus don't claim particular denominations, sects differ by the primary deity they worship, though they don't deny the divinity of other gods. This was true despite the fact that each tradition had different versions of the same stories, like the tale of Sita and Ram. (Nina Paley's 2008 animated film, *Sita Sings the Blues*, is a beautifully-rendered illustration of the many interpretations of this single tale.)

While the open-hearted approach to worship was compelling, I didn't take the legends any more literally than I did biblical ones. And like Christianity, Hinduism has played a role in preserving racism and classicism, making that theology as objectionable to me as any other.

"We are glad you are joining us now," Ramana smiled. "Any day of the Kumbh is a good day for bathing in the Ganges."

"We're heading straight to the river? To bathe?" *What about the holy man Preeti mentioned?*

Preeti smiled. "Yes, aren't we fortunate?"

Are we?

ARE YOU MY GURU?

Uttar Pradesh, 2013

Ramana adjusted the voluminous white scarf he wore over his butter yellow sweater. "These so-called 'auspicious days,'" he said. "They just create unnecessary problems."

Maybe he thought the shocked look on my face owed to lingering fears about the footbridge collapse, but I was far more worried about the water. Ramana's willingness to reject the ceremony, however, was also a surprise. Far more open-minded than I'd imagined possible for any priest given that the bathing dates were set by the pandits. Maybe Ramana could be my guru.

But this would turn out to be our longest conversation.

Preeti, Ramana, and the rest chatted away in Hindi. Not that I felt left out. There was too much to see—more tents and caravans, people sleeping in open air, stray animals, and chai wallahs making and selling spicy tea on the side of the road. I would've loved to stop for some, but we seemed to be in a hurry so I didn't ask. When we made it to the riverbank, we followed Ramana onto a wooden pier that appeared to be suspended on giant balloons. Were we supposed to just hop in?

My four companions, however, made no such moves to jump, instead keeping up their steady banter. Presently a pontoon boat came along, and the group sprang into action, boarding the boat at once. Preeti and Ramana on one side, Padma, Ashima, and me on the other.

"Look at the water," Ramana said, pointing into the murky, solid-colored wet. "You can see the different colors of the Ganges and the Yamuna."

Though I've since seen this phenomenon illustrated in photos, in person I saw no contrast in the water. But Ramana was satisfied. He sat back and began to hum lightly, until we came to a halt.

"We are at the sangam, the holiest spot," Padma said, leaning toward me as suddenly, Ramana began to strip. He was discrete—removing his garments beneath the voluminous white fabric he'd worn around his neck—but still. Were we supposed to do the same? I didn't have a scarf. And was I even getting in this water reportedly not fit for bathing dogs?

"This is the holy confluence," Padma said, unstrapping her Dior sandal. "You must dip yourself three times in the water."

Now Ramana was deftly fashioning his scarf into swimwear.

Three *dunks?*

The number reminded me of Buddhist prostrations. Or

the Father, Son, and Holy Spirit. Why did we fight about these interpretations? We can barely translate each other, let alone the divine. We were all as wrong as we were right.

By now the group was in the Ganges. Without another thought I removed my footwear just as Preeti, Padma, and Ashima had done, and jumped into the water. The air temperature hovered around sixty degrees Fahrenheit and the water temperature couldn't have been much higher. Yet despite my lifelong aversion to cold, I felt comfortable in the water, rejuvenated. The five of us spent a good half-hour, dunking and floating in what appeared to be clear water.

On the return ride Ramana softly sang ancient mantras while the rest of us sat in silence. Fairly certain we'd peaked, I was keen for a rest, but no. We stopped in front of a tent where we were guided past the line and directly to seats in the front row.

Of course! Ramana was a priest from one of India's holiest cities. He had to be one of the country's holiest men.

A pair of government officials came into the tent, and, as the five of us sat in silence, still dripping, we watched the two unironically discuss the need for a cleaner Ganges. Then a ruckus sounded outside.

Ramana signaled us to follow and we rushed across the way to an even bigger tent, where our pandit was given a seat at the front of the room. A hush fell over the crowd as a procession made its way in and an enormous man was brought in on a tasseled litter and deposited next to Ramana.

The man, I later discovered, was Swami Swaroo-
panand Saraswati, one of the four holiest men in India.
Not long before this, he'd threatened to boycott the
Kumbh, citing a lack of adequate space, but I couldn't
have said if his aloof manner owed to his complaint or
was just his way. Though he and Ramana sat side-by-
side, they didn't speak. Devotees rushed to touch the
Swami's feet. The Swami yawned. At one point he took a
phone call. Then, as mysteriously as our visit had begun,
Ramana's appointment was deemed over and we were
practically pushed from the room.

"Now this is an auspicious day," Ramana said,
delighted.

From there we toured every hot spot at the Kumbh.
He knew where everything was happening, as well as,
somehow, the schedule. We rode from tent to tent
listening to holy men in saffron robes, none of whom I
understood.

Along the dirt paths, vendors hawked everything from
prayer beads to children's games. The vibe was
somewhere between Miami beach and a rave, only
everyone was on the prowl for spirituality instead of
MDMA. There were crowds and bullhorns, but—unlike I
would at a crowded beach party—I felt calm and
peaceful.

We returned to our ashram to find the mantra
marathon still underway. Prayers were called out, after
which the white-clad adherents would chant, "SVA-ha!"
Then throw what looked like rice into the fire. Preeti and
the gang were going to some ceremony at Ramana's tent,
leaving me to fend for myself that evening.

Sure I'd never get any sleep with all the racket, I took a walk around the compound. The chanting was at the center of the interior courtyard, a square of canvas shelters housing sleeping quarters, a full kitchen and dining area, as well as toilet facilities with running water. *So, this is what it's like to glamp.*

Near the check-in, I found a schedule showing that dinner would be served soon. Even if I couldn't fall asleep, I could do a relaxation meditation, the kind I loved teaching my students. I'd barely removed my shoes before I fell into a deep sleep on my cot.

The sound of my roommate returning woke me. A new day had dawned and she'd been out working already.

"I hope I didn't wake you," she said. "It's only six-thirty."

I slept for ten hours?

"You were out when I got in last night," she smiled. Though the room held four cots, she was the only other person sharing the space. "Hi, I'm Madhya."

I introduced myself. "That's an interesting name, where are you from?"

"Oh, it's not my given name, it's the name I chose here. It means Middle Way," she smiled. As the sleep cleared from my eyes, I saw that Madhya—like the people around the fire—was dressed in a white robe and, in addition to her robe, a white turban. "I'm from Houston."

"Oh," I said, unsure how to connect. I wanted to know more about the ashram's guru—she was obviously a follower and I was obviously not—but I didn't want to start off too aggressively. "I have a friend who lives there.

She loves it. When did you get to the Kumbh?"

"From the beginning. I helped build this shelter," she said. "I thought I loved teaching yoga, which is what I did in Houston, but this has been the best experience of my life."

Usually, I'd at least mention that I also taught yoga, but something told me if I wanted to get any intel, I had to stay on track.

"How did you find this teacher? She looks like she could be from Hawaii. Is that why she attracts so many Westerners?"

Madhya smiled. "There aren't many Western people at the Kumbh Mela, you're right. I'm not sure why guruji's teachings resonate with so many of us, but here." She pressed a slim book into my hand.

I could read later; I wanted answers. "What do you like most about her teaching?"

Madhya was nodding, as if she'd been expecting my questions. "She calls if you're drawn."

Her non-answers were maddening, but I held out hope, pointing my thumb toward the courtyard choir. "What are they praying for?"

"It's a puja for the *blahblahblahah-asanan*," she said in, I guessed, Sanskrit.

Talking to Madhya was like consulting the dictionary and finding that the word you don't know is printed there as the definition of itself. I changed topics.

"Did you bathe in the river?"

"On the first day, yes." Her skin flushed.

"The only time you've been in the Ganges was day one?" So much for tact.

"Well, it took us hours to reach Mother Ganga."

I didn't know what to say. Sharing my experience would've felt like a not-so-humble brag. "What was that like?"

"By the time we reached the holy water, I was eager for something cool on my body," she paused, a look of rapture crossing her face. "I only had a moment to douse myself before I had to let the next person in, but the experience was so beautiful I practically floated home."

"Would you go back? Maybe take a longer swim?"

"I would love to visit with Mother again before I go," she said. "But I'm very busy here..." She trailed off, looking around, seemingly dazed.

Was she all right? I tried a practical follow-up. "Will you head back to Houston when the Kumbh is over?"

"I'm not sure," she replied, still dreamy.

Before I could think what to ask next, she picked up her bucket of toiletries and headed for the shower.

"Enjoy your stay," she said by way of goodbye. I would not see her again.

Looking into my palm, I hoped the text she'd handed me might provide useful intel, but it was a copy of Patanjali's yoga sutras, widely available everywhere. *I guess she didn't think I got the call.*

After my shower and a delicious breakfast of fruit and yogurt, I looked for Preeti and the others again but they were nowhere to be found. I waited awhile, listening to the chanting and drinking tea before realizing I was on my own and ratcheted up the courage to wander away from camp. My goal was to not get lost while also actively staying on the lookout for potential gurus.

The easiest possibilities to dismiss were the random sadhus. Scattered about the grounds in various states of undress, these men showed their devotion by keeping an arm held high, letting their fingernails grow for life, or lying on beds of nails. They weren't looking for followers so much as attention. I wondered, Had my solution become another problem? Had I been pursuing spirituality like another addiction?

Then there were the big tents lit up with enormous Om signs and festooned with speakers. Beyond pushed-aside canvas were rows of folding chairs facing a podium where non-Western teachers taught in non-Western languages.

The search would've felt like a bust if it weren't for the general atmosphere, which had a profound effect. Everyone was here hoping to connect more deeply with the sacred. Looking around, I recalled a passage from Thomas Merton's *Conjectures of a Guilty Bystander*. In it, Merton is out shopping when he realizes that trying to live as a monk separate from the world is folly. The people he sees aren't strangers, they're the same as him. When he sees their "secret beauty," he wonders what would happen if everyone had the same vision. He writes: "I suppose the big problem would be that we would fall down and worship each other."

Later at the tent, I reconnected with Preeti.

"I missed you all today," I said as we hugged. "Listen, I can't thank you enough for arranging all this. It's incredible."

"Come! See our room!"

I was pleasantly surprised by the invitation; as a group they'd been fairly reserved, which made it all the more unexpected to find Ashima and Padma there, in a space similar to mine, giggling like teenagers.

"Stop! Naa? Lisa will think we are mad!" Preeti admonished, before erupting in giggles.

When the laughter died down, Ashima spoke up. "We have just returned from the other… *accommodation*."

More laughter. This time Padma spoke up. "Miss Lisa, thank *you* so much."

"Thank me? What for?"

"Padma-ji, she doesn't know what you mean," Preeti said, then turned to me. "We're happy because last night and today we went to a ceremony where Ramana is staying. Where we were going to stay. Let's just say…"

"Horrible!" said Ashima.

And again, they all broke down laughing.

"If we hadn't met," Preeti said. "That's where we'd be right now."

"First we were disappointed—"

"Ashima!"

"Well, it's true. We don't get to see Ramana like this very often, and we were looking forward to spending time with him," Ashima said. "But he thought you would be more comfortable if we were all together."

"Oh no," I said, shocked to realize how dramatically I'd changed their plans. "I'm so sorry."

"No no," said Padma. "His tent did not have running water."

"No toilets!" Ashima said.

"I would not have wanted to eat their food," said Preeti. "Staying there would've been terrible."

"And the beds!" Ashima looked at her friends. "There weren't any! We would've been sleeping on the floor."

"I don't think Ramana-ji would want to be our pandit anymore if we'd stayed there," Padma laughed.

They weren't just being kind, they meant it. They even invited me to stay with them in Mumbai. But I had to get back to Goa. I'd just made arrangements to visit a sex ashram.

THE SEX ASHRAM

Karnataka, 2013

Before leaving Goa for the Kumbh, I'd been in Jenny's shop perusing the merch with Debra—she of the teacher training course's "Best Bollywood Style" award—and wondering if Jenny's invitation to work in the shop had been a better opportunity than teaching after all. Previously a single shelf at the check-in window, the store was now a separate room and stood adjacent to the shala's covered concrete practice area. Clothing racks and shelves lining the walls burst with yoga gear.

Debra had just slung a turquoise yoga mat bag over her shoulder. True to the award she'd been given at our yoga teacher training, Debra remained a fashion icon. I, on the other hand, had stopped having accidents. *Progress*, I let her presence remind me.

"Love that," I said, tapping Debra's mat bag. "Want to go for breakfast?"

Before we'd settled on a place, Jenny joined us.

"Oh good," she said. "I'm glad you're both here."

Intriguing.

"I remember you mentioned Osho when you were here last time," she said. "I just saw they're offering a Family Constellation workshop."

I had? I remembered learning about the place back in Qatar, from one of the Brits in my yoga class.

"If you're going to India," my student had urged before knocking back a finger of whiskey, "you should go to Osho."

We were at a bar after yoga because bars were where all the expats socialized and by then I'd announced I was leaving my job to study yoga in India. I talked about the possible options freely.

"What's *AW-show*?" I'd asked, unintentionally mimicking Anthony's pronunciation of the guru more widely known in the U.S. as OH-show.

Anthony described the place as an ashram in Pune, India. "They run therapeutic courses throughout the year. Meditation, chakra healing, family constellation, you name it."

"Family constellation?" I asked, not because I was unfamiliar with this family therapy technique, but because it had been on my radar for years, ever since a friend in recovery had told me about her experience. Her description—sessions where a group of people acted out family dynamics, as in role-played—sent me straight to the editor at the newspaper where I was a regular contributor.

"Family constellation would be a great story," I'd

enthused. "I mean, is it therapy or improv?"

Sadly, he didn't feel the same. I never did go, but I'd never forgotten my question. The technique was unlike anything I'd heard of, let alone tried.

Before Anthony answered, my yoga teacher—also out with us—rolled her eyes and shifted in her chair. "That place is a full-on sex ashram. You have to take an AIDS test just to get in."

"Who is dumb enough to think that's in any way preventative?" I asked, ever the diplomat.

"Yes, well, Osho left his body in 1990, at the height of the AIDS crisis," Anthony said. "But Osho is about so much more."

I wasn't convinced and so lost interest in attending, though apparently I'd not forgotten about Osho either.

Jenny continued. "Did you ever get to Osho the last time you were here?"

I shook my head.

"I didn't think so," Jenny said, putting her hand on Debra's arm. "Didn't you just get back?"

"Yes!" Debra now hugged the mat bag. "You should totally go."

I hesitated. Debra had just been to the sex ashram? It hadn't been all that long since—after relating how I'd come to date through adult websites—she'd asked, "Don't you worry about disease?" I was flabbergasted. If she and her husband had sex as infrequently as I managed to get lucky, I suspected they'd be heading to divorce court. *Didn't she know about safe sex?* Which pointed to my current hesitation.

"What about…" I began, unsure how to complete my

sentence. After leaving Qatar the first time, I'd dropped the idea of Osho worried that random sex would do less to heal my wounds than rip up the scabs. And while I was no longer so afraid of being hurt, my mind filled with visions of furry-toed men in Birkenstocks pawing at me.

"You mean the whole sex ashram thing?" Jenny finished my thought.

"Yes!"

"Oh, there's no pressure at all," Debra smiled. "You don't have to have sex with anyone."

Don't have to? But did you? I wanted to ask.

Jenny tightened her ponytail. "Let's do it. There's a course starting at the end of the month, just after this teacher training ends."

"I'll be back from the Kumbh Mela by then," I said, having told everyone in earshot my plans.

"I can't believe you're going," Jenny said, which made me feel like a rock star but in hindsight just might've been a warning. "I'll book us a room straightaway, the places around there fill up."

Osho, the place, was named after Osho, the man. Born Chandra Mohan Jain in Raisen, India, the man who would become Osho was initially called Acharya Rajneesh by his followers. Then Bhagwan Sri Rajneesh. And then finally, the eponymous guru. His message was to love. Everybody. And as often as possible. More formally, he espoused the idea that orgasm was the meditative state closest to godliness because one loses the sense of self, attaining the state of no mind. Having multiple partners

229

eliminated false boundaries and presumably ensured more godliness. This made him extremely popular.

But—to paraphrase my friend Anthony—Osho had other ideas too. "Be realistic," he said. "Plan for a miracle." Also, "Creativity is the greatest rebellion in existence." And, "Friendship is the purest love."

Though I agreed with much of what Osho espoused—and had certainly been empowered through sexual encounters—as philosophies went, I found the idea of orgasm as the godliest state puerile. Willy was right. I did want a Higher Power I could access in all circumstances, but sexual energy was not what I wanted to take to grocery stores or job interviews. This was probably why I'd never related to those S.L.A.A. groups—my longing for an intimate partner was not for the sake of acquiring love. And while admittedly I still believed an intimate partner showed proof of healing, my main desire was to find a partner interested in growth.

With the right partner, my life would be bigger. We would help each other grow. I could reconcile myself to the idea of being single, but that was not the same as eschewing love.

The answer was, indeed, more spirituality. More love.

Having decided not to attend Osho previously, I'd stopped my research. Thus I knew nothing of his commune in Oregon or that he'd been deported from the U.S. in 1985 for violating immigration laws. Nor did I have any knowledge about his American flock, which was accused that same year—and later convicted—of trying to take over their town by means of murder (salmonella poisoning, to be precise). I don't know if I'd have canceled my trip had I learned this information, but I'm glad I didn't have to find out.

Jenny and I met up in Mumbai where she'd already spent a week doing a panchakarma cleanse. As we traveled together by car to Pune, we compared notes on cleanses—I'd done one in Bengaluru on my first trip—but soon fell into silence as our driver salmoned through the densely packed streets.

"How can you be so calm?" I asked Jenny, placidly scrolling through her phone.

She looked up. "I figure, if it's my time to die, it's my time. Stressing isn't going to change anything."

I nodded. It was probably best I'd never worked for her.

The hotel Jenny had booked was just down the road from Osho, which billed itself as a "meditation resort." This was long before Goop (Gwyneth Paltrow's pseudoscience lifestyle company) made that sound like something other than an oxymoron.

Our plan was to drop our bags, zip over to the ashram to get our bearings, then escape the orgiastic pleasure dome until we absolutely had to return for class. Though Jenny hadn't said why she wanted to go to Osho, she'd made it clear she wasn't looking for casual hookups any more than I was.

As our driver rolled into Pune's pollution-choked roads, we saw smoking pyres of garbage consisting of, among other things, plastic water bottles. I wasn't sure I'd survive the short trek from our hotel to Osho. The impending blood test did nothing to strengthen my resolve.

Osho's HIV testing center was a shipping container-like box that sat in front of the gate, the only part of Osho visible from the street. The campus was concealed behind a wall of bamboo.

We entered the windowless space to await our turn for a blood draw. How did they handle the test takers who "failed?" Could there be a worse way to find out you were HIV positive?

Near as I could tell, everyone in our group "passed." We didn't get results so much as permission to enter en masse, by way of the Osho gift shop, a clever placement that also ensured visitors maintained the Osho dress code.

While on the Osho campus, maroon robes were to be worn at all times (except during certain meditations, which required all white). Queasy as I felt at the prospect of running around in burgundy—not my color—the robes were the sole aspect of this venture that struck me as remotely ashram-like, a stripping away of the outer trappings to focus on the individual. Or so I thought until I spied the wares.

The women's display looked like a stall at a Renaissance Festival, complete with lace-up bustiers and frilly adornments. Not a style that suits my blocky body. I had to purchase something—I was fresh out of purple gowns—I don't like to shop in general, but particularly not under mandatory pressure.

Eventually I found an acceptably plain garment, a

dress that reminded me of a Halloween costume my mother once made—a triangle of a witch's robe with bell sleeves and a full, ankle-length skirt. *If this doesn't discourage lechers nothing will.*

At the register I found maroon thongs and blindfolds in baskets; this was feeling less ashram-like all the time. Resort-approved garb on my back and fear of Lotharios on my mind, I gritted my teeth and entered Osho, determined to stick to plan. We'd case the grounds, and escape immediately.

Across the threshold, the contrast was stark. Unlike the streets of Pune, Osho was a lush, Dr. Seuss-like environment, generously planted with tropical vegetation and decorated with water features that provided a calming soundtrack. Between the resort's pool, three vegetarian cafes, and bookstore, the only reason to leave was to sleep at our hotel or venture up to the German Bakery for morning coffee. Those brief forays would be more than enough.

We spent the afternoon by the water, alternately lounging, reading, and eating, leaving only when the pool closed.

THE BEST MOVIE YOU EVER SAW

Karnataka, 2013

The next morning, we rose early to grab coffees at the German Bakery before heading to our first family constellation session. The café was a sea of maroon.

"Which course are you taking?" I asked the robed man in front of me as we waited in line.

"Course? What do you mean? I always dress like this."

I laughed, noting that he wasn't wearing Birkenstocks. His dark hair and beard had a salty tinge. He looked about my age—certainly younger than the creepy olds I'd imagined— and slightly taller than me.

The three of us chatted a while, exchanging details. When she wasn't running the shala in Goa, Jenny taught in the U.K. and brought groups to Goa. Hugh was a therapist from Findhorn.

"Give me your number and I'll text you," Hugh said. "We can alternate coffee runs." The doorbell jangled as he left with his coffee.

I looked at Jenny. "Where's Finndorn?" I asked, imagining it was spelled how it sounded.

"It's a New Age healing community in Scotland, pretty much like this place," Jenny said as we got our drinks.

There were more places like this? Maybe I'd go there someday.

"Not sure why he'd come here, though."

"I can see it," I said. "You wouldn't want to do training at that shala would you?"

Jenny's face went slack. "I take classes there all the time."

Noted.

During the previous day's visit, we'd found a community bulletin board where schedules and upcoming classes were posted. Other than the homespun approach to information dissemination, the schedule was surprisingly business-like for a sex cult—eight hours of workshops with a lunch break in the middle.

We headed straight to our class and found a circle of chairs and I exhaled, relieved we wouldn't be on the floor. There were twenty of us, all from different parts of the globe.

"Family constellation is a way of bringing people in contact with love," our leader began. He spoke slowly, with a rhythmic accent that might've been German or Israeli. His name, Svagito, wasn't much of a clue because it was his sannyasin name, the one he would've received on becoming an Oshoite. His frame was slender and he had curly gray hair ringing his otherwise bald pate. Whatever his background, Svagito was—if not handsome—terribly compelling.

"This is what drew me to the practice, after many years of family therapy, because by nature, I'm a very critical and judgmental person."

He did not come across as critical or judgmental in the least.

"How the constellation works, nobody knows. People say it is energy. Morphokinetic. But we don't know. I like that. Not knowing is as close to love as you can get. When you want to know, you are moving far away from the answer."

Heat rose in my body. Wanting to know had defined my entire healing quest. Was this where I'd gone wrong?

Svagito went on to explain his method, explaining that we wouldn't be called on. Rather, we'd volunteer to tell our stories and allow the process to unfold. Once we described our issue, Svagito would call the other participants to the center of the circle where we'd move ourselves around. "Let the energy of the circle guide you," Svagito instructed.

What if I didn't feel guided?

"Through family constellation, we begin to see the mother. The father. The grandparents."

I went from mild panic to judge-y in a heartbeat. *So heteronormative.* Though I'd been married to a man and

236

exclusively heterosexual since, I'd been with both men and women. Mentally, I hadn't ruled out any possibilities

"When I see the generations," Svagito went on, "my heart opens. Effortlessly. There is no trying. This is natural. This is what love should be."

Effortless loving? What a joy that would be. *I will try to overlook the gendered language.*

And in this way, nod by nod, my stony resistance began to crumble.

The first person up was a petite, dark-haired Iranian woman. When she raised her hand, Svagito called her to the center of the circle. Recalling the sight of army rebels kidnapping her father, she trembled, breaking down after telling us, "I've never seen him since."

Svagito was nonreactive. "You are not now in danger, yes," he commanded, his voice not unkind but also not connecting with her pain. The woman's sobbing stopped short. When she continued, Svagito asked questions without ever interrupting. "Tell me who was left. Brothers? Sisters?"

Calling on volunteers, Svagito chose whoever raised their hand regardless of gender, bucking my concerns over bias. I joined the circle. And it happened. Somehow, I felt guided.

"The first love is for the mother," Svagito said. "And it is very powerful. When we fall in love, we seek to recreate that union."

As the session went on, the emotional release was pervasive, whether it was the person at the center or someone moving within the constellation, emotions ran high throughout. Anyone might cry. The workshop continued in this way for days, unraveling cosmopolitan tales of genocide, homicide, and suicide. Benign as they might begin, the stories often took a turn. One woman complained how she always picked the wrong men, but soon Svagito's questions uncovered how, as a child, she'd seen her father kill her mother.

My divorce? An issue? When he began a new circle, I kept my hand in my lap. I was letting go of plenty as a participant. *Nothing wrong here.*

Hugh met us for lunch at Osho's al fresco cafe.

"Oh, hey, Amir!" Hugh stood and waved over a young man I recognized from our course.

Though Jenny, Hugh, and I were all in our early forties, Amir looked to be in his early twenties. Before he even said hello, I guessed from his closely cropped hair and fit physique that he'd just finished his year of military service in Israel; India was a popular post-conscription landing pad.

"How are you liking the constellation work?" Hugh asked once Amir was situated with his tray.

"It's very different to the craniosacral course. All outward." Amir forked his couscous salad but stopped before taking a bite. "Each session takes about an hour. You think you'd get bored, but..." He looked up, his deep brown eyes serious. "It's like watching the best movie you ever saw. All day long."

His rich laughter spread through the group and the

conversation flowed easily.

"Anyone want to run up to the German Bakery for coffee?" I asked as lunch wrapped up.

"Oh, no," said Hugh. "You must come to the Buddha Grove."

The Buddha Grove was an open-air pavilion that accommodated lectures and yoga classes, and concerts as well as lunchtime DJs who played Ibiza-style dance music. From our first lunch, every day at midday, Jenny, Hugh, Amir, and I would join the robed throng and sway to the chill lounge beats. At night we split up, heading to various talks or meditations, or to dance or swim or eat. Often as not, we'd reconnect at the German Bakery in the morning.

One evening, Amir and I decided to take a swim. En route to the pool, a bookstore display caught my attention. "What are those?" I asked Amir, pointing to a pile labeled "Datebooks."

Amir's eyes followed my fingertip to the display and back to me. "They are datebooks." He grinned, melting me.

Though I wasn't generally attracted when there was that much of an age gap or particularly to Amir, between all the swimming, dancing, and emoting, I wasn't surprised to feel momentarily turned on. The kid was objectively good-looking. Looking back at the display to catch my breath, I went on. "I can see that but there aren't any calendars. The pages are all blank."

"Ah," he said, still smiling. "They're for keeping your rendezvous straight. Here, a *date* means sex. If someone asks you for a date, it is to make love."

My neck flushed. No one was asking me on dates.

"Only I could come to a sex ashram, afraid of lecherous advances," I told Jenny later that night in our room. "And then be annoyed when no one came on to me!"

"I feel the same!" she said.

I looked at her, wide-eyed. Though neither of us was interested in flings, I'd convinced myself she would've had something juicy to report; her gift shop purchase had a fitted bodice that showed off her lovely cleavage.

Normally I'd have been all up in my roomie's business about who she was hooking up with, but Jenny was my teacher. Since teaching yoga was our profession, we were more associates than buddies. And since the conversation with Debra, where she'd mysteriously slut-shamed me then fucked off to Osho herself, I'd grown more reticent.

Now that this conversation with Jenny was underway, however, I felt empowered to probe. Everything about Osho induced arousal and intimacy. It was weirder not to discuss our desires openly.

"What about Hugh?" If they didn't have such a great rapport, I might've gone for him.

Jenny squinted and I braced myself; I'd learned to read disapproval before I learned to read. "What would I want with a public-school boy?"

Her insult was a very British swipe at Hugh's unacceptable level of privilege. Though I understood the snark, I didn't see a callous disregard for others in him. He was a therapist, after all.

"I'd be more into Amir," she smiled. "But he's just so…"

"Young!" we both said, laughing. Had I not been in a family therapy workshop, I likely would've missed the significance of our conversation, but by lunch the next day, I wasn't looking at Hugh the same way. My attraction had diminished.

Later that same afternoon, Svagito closed the day's session with a truth bomb. "Because of your aunt's sickness, your mother felt unloved," he said to the man at the center of the constellation, pointing out how the participants had shifted within a space. "She withheld because she didn't want you to become dependent on her. Consequently, your need for her approval grew stronger. This is the dynamic you keep playing out with lovers."

His words applied to the situation I was in with Hugh.

My mother was like the cool beautiful girl I couldn't get on the right side of, and I'd often felt the same about my ex when we were married, that he was too good for me and I had to keep working to win his approval. When it came to the current situation, Jenny was the cool girl, and my need to please her overrode my attraction for Hugh. I put her thoughts and feelings above my own just like I've done with my mother, my ex, and countless others, attempting to gain approval and make myself worthy of their love.

Go where it's warm.

Quite po33333ssibly a platitude I'd read on a mug, but in that moment those words came to mind and resonated. If I wanted to stop throwing myself at the mercy of cold, less-than-fulfilling relationships, it was up to me.

Our workshop was wrapping up and I couldn't avoid my turn any longer. As I mumbled through my story, I tried to sexy the plot up as one of stealth intercontinental divorce. Svagito saw right through me. Quickly mapping out my family, he put Amir in the role of my father.

I stood awkwardly in the center, between him and the woman playing my mother, who immediately moved in front of the man playing my sister.

Typical, I thought. Mom always did like Tess more than me.

"It is you who is doing the rejecting," Svagito concluded. My constellation was over.

In what I now know is a classic trauma response—and nothing like the fraction of time available to redirect before responding out of habit—my mind blanked. By the time I was back in my body, Svagito was wrapping up his concluding remarks and I was actively rejecting.

Whatthehell? How could I have refused my parents? Or my ex? Preposterous!

And yet all week, Svagito had been nailing issue after issue. If I couldn't make sense of what he said, I feared that the final, most crucial, lesson was simply beyond my reach. When the session ended, I marched out of class and headed straight for the community bulletin board where I'd been tempted by another course, the three-day Tantra Experience. Conveniently, class was scheduled to start the next day.

THE KISS OF TANTRA

Bangalore, 2013

My roommate was still asleep when I awoke the next morning, anxious about the coming workshop. I slipped out of the room alone and made my way to the coffee shop, but still had to drag myself to my seat, reluctant to discover more truths.

"My beloveds," purred our incredibly hot Italian leader, Sambhavo. "During this week, we ask that you not have any dates. Not with anyone on the course or outside."

No sex? During a Tantra workshop? Was he joking?

But he was not kidding. Of course he was not.

"Tantra," Sambhavo said, "is about saying yes to *what is*. Letting go of our conditioned responses."

Leaving would only prove how right Svagito had been. Not that my motivation for staying was strictly to prove him wrong. I wanted to stop rejecting. It didn't hurt that Sambhavo's curly dark hair brushed his square jaw at an intriguing angle. I wanted to run my fingertips along that line.

I was hooked from the first exercise, a series of dance moves Sambhavo led us through, designed to evoke our masculine and feminine sides. To use gender—as opposed to being trapped by its supposed inevitability—soothed the skeptic in me, opening the door to more acceptance.

At the heart of Sambhavo's teaching was Osho's message of love.

"We speak of falling in love," Sambhavo said. "But why? Energetically, that feels terrible. We should rise in love."

Osho, Sambhavo explained, didn't advocate random sex partners so much as he wanted his followers to feel love, both as a giver and receiver. That was a new take on Osho, and sounded more like Willy, or even Ricky. Was this how Love had become my Higher Power, all the loving I'd been doing?

"We should not designate a special someone," he said. "Learning to love everyone is ultimately a sexless state."

Ongoing celibacy? He couldn't mean that. We were in a Tantra class at a sex cult. Plus, I wanted my special someone. *Objection!* I thought, and had to laugh at myself.

Endlessly seeking a single spiritual path had kept me locked in the hunt for imperfections. But I'd decided I wanted to follow Love. Why not take a polytheistic approach and borrow whatever methods helped in that pursuit?

That afternoon, when I returned to the lobby to retrieve my key, I was told I'd been checked out. I'd known Jenny was heading back to Goa before me, but not exactly when. I'd figured I'd just extend my stay in the room, but my bags were behind the desk.

"Sorry, madam, the room is booked," the slender young man behind the counter said.

"No problem," I was determined to love everything. "May I book another?"

"Sorry, madam," he yes/no nodded. "We are fully booked."

Lisa, you fucking moron—

I stopped myself abruptly. No point in wasting time abusing myself. I flipped open my mobile and pressed the first contact that popped up: Amir.

"I just ordered pizza," he said. "Come on over."

Amir was at an apartment nearby, one I soon learned featured an outdoor deck, a modern kitchen, and a living room with a flat-screen TV. I grabbed a slice and happily joined my new roommate on the couch in front of a movie. Before long, I was violating the rules of my Tantra workshop. Until I halted the proceedings.

"You have condoms, right? You know the whole AIDS test thing is bullshit in terms of protection."

Amir grinned. "Of course."

The sex was adequate, better than with Ricky anyway. But I wasn't in any way drawn to Amir. In the aftermath, tears fell from my eyes.

Amir brushed the salty tracks from my face, but his

comfort felt worse. I didn't want his consolation, I wanted to get away. He fell asleep holding me, but my predicament kept me awake. I didn't want to be in bed with someone who didn't know that tears weren't part of my lovemaking repertoire. Or were they? Had I turned into someone who cried after a shag?

Instead of scorching myself with criticism, I took the opportunity to sit with my feelings. Though the free-floating suicidal ideations had stopped, I'd remained prone to weeping fits and still the occasional, barbarous, self-critique.

Post-coital tears can't be my new normal, I thought. *Wait, am I rejecting?*

The thought made me laugh. Not only was I seeing the stories I told, I was putting them into perspective.

Once I'd reframed the incident as a lapse and not an indictment, I was overwhelmed by an urgent need to leave Amir's apartment. Anything to avoid further contact. With all the earnest dialoguing that was the Osho experience, I was liable to report what I'd discovered. There's no good way to tell someone you're just not into them.

Once I broke free from Amir's building, I came face-to-face with the dark night. Very dark. There were no 24-hour shops or all-night diners. There were very few lights. I feared for my safety.

Without thinking much about it, I found my fingers dialing for Hugh. "Come over," he said.

Retreat pro that he was, Hugh had a place *on* the Osho campus. In short order, I once again found myself violating the Tantra workshop rules, only this time with no tears. Far from it.

I didn't know Hugh any better than Amir, but we could talk. And talk. Hugh made for an exceptional lover—responsive, generous, fun—and more. As we greeted the dawn, Hugh tenderly washed my hair over a bucket, an act of intimacy I'd never before experienced. Might this be the start of something?

The Tantra workshop became punctuation to my sessions with Hugh. Now that I had my someone special, I was even more into the lessons.

"Your whole energy is released in loving," Sambhavo told us. "Being playfully sensuous without holding yourself back, without any fear, is one of the greatest blessings to humanity. Sensuousness is consciousness filtering through the body."

How were these other people not having sex? As the days wore on, I felt restored. Not because I'd found "true love," but because I was fostering my capacity to adore.

In one exercise, Sambhavo had us lie on the floor, knees bent, while one person sat at our heels and another at our head. While imagining a situation that hadn't gone to plan—I went with my marriage—we were to visualize the energy moving through our chakras and express the experience audibly. Not with words but sound. Sambhavo joined us, so it was only after this part of the class ended that I learned he hadn't attended each group.

"You were very loud," my exercise partner told me later. To my ears, I'd sounded the same as the others.

During other lessons, we'd sit on the floor in pairs, cross-legged and eye-to-eye, one hand on our partner's hearts. We might sit this way in silence or speak. "Be sincere. Love as much as you can. Enjoy your sensuality," Sambhavo said as he danced between the couples.

At the day's end, I couldn't wait to play these games with Hugh and take them to their logical, sexual conclusion.

Our final class exercise was a dry-hump orgy that Sambhavo called an "energy circle." The men in the class stood, encircling the women on the floor. I cannot recall quite how we went from eye gazing to writhing together, if the overtly sexual touch was guided or spontaneous, but that was what happened. And I was into it, groping through the loving embrace of the beauteous women who'd exposed their tenderest selves and allowed me to do the same.

"Traditions have been against expressiveness because a person who is expressive cannot be enslaved," Sambhavo told us. "He lives according to his own nature."

Hugh stayed on at Osho, but I headed back to Goa when the Tantra course ended. Even as I exhorted him to visit, I didn't need or expect him to. Knowing he wanted to was enough. Nor did I mind knowing he might have someone else in his bed that very day.

I was getting the hang of this love thing.

THE PSYCHIC
MEGAPHONE

Goa, 2013

Development had come to Goa since my first visit. Many of the roads had been widened to accommodate tour buses, and there were an astonishing number of concrete block projects under construction. All of which made me appreciate the older properties like the one Jenny found me, an old stone mansion topped by a red tile roof, an enormous structure built to protect inhabitants from monsoons.

"Welcome to Hercules Manor," Emma said when I'd arrived at the house in Goa, fixing me with a stare from her saucer-like cobalt eyes. All Jenny had told me about my roommates, other than the fact that they were doing a course at her shala, was that they were from the U.K.

"Hercules?" I asked, wondering if this was some

British thing. "Because it's big?"

"No, silly!" said Nicola, my other new roommate. Unlike most yoginis, Nicola kept her copper-brown hair cropped close. She stood at least a head and shoulders over me and cast an imposing shadow, coming across as someone who didn't tolerate deviation. "There's only one bathroom and no hot water. You've got to have real strength to live here."

"I'm so glad you came forward," Emma said. "That nose-picking Megan was our other option."

The lack of hot water was not unusual, but I should've seen the cliquish remark as a warning. Instead, I reveled in being part of a girl gang. So it was a real shock when, on my return from Osho, I found myself wondering who'd moved things around in my room.

I'd only just passed my roommates on the way to my room moments earlier. Neither Nicola nor Emma had said a word. My suspicion that someone had been sleeping in my bed couldn't be right. Then I saw it—a single strand of dark, curly hair on my pillowcase. Not a match to me, or crop-haired Nicola, or blonde Emma.

"Hey guys," I yelled downstairs. "Was someone in my room while I was away?"

"Oh yeah," answered Emma, like she'd never considered this might be of interest. "We let Tom stay a few nights."

I ran down to the dining room where she and Nicola sat, splitting a piece of cruelty-free, vegan cake.

"A few *nights*? In my *bed*?"

"You don't mind, do you," Nicola said/asked without bothering to look my way. I found her domineering even when she wasn't being haughty, which was never.

Emma blew on her tea, regarding me over the rim, drawing a line in steam.

Of course, I minded. But the idea that I could be angry and right was not something I'd allowed myself to consider just yet. Though I'd seen her uses, I was still ashamed of my Inner Bitch. Between the accountability tenets I'd learned in recovery and the "love everyone" ideals I was trying to live, if I was angry I feared I was not only wrong but about to be ejected from polite society in much the same way I'd been ejected from my marriage. Ergo, I should not be angry. If I felt angry? *Swallow it.* It's a wonder my stomach didn't explode, but I suppose my tears provided a slow-drip release.

As I watched Nicola and Emma sip tea and munch on cake, I asked myself the three questions I'd learned in Al Anon (the recovery program for people whose lives are touched by addiction):

Does it need to be said by me?

Does it need to be said?

Does it need to be said right now?

For sure I was the only person who would bring this up, but I wasn't sure about the need for voicing my concern. There was no changing the fact that Tom had slept in my room, and besides, Nicola and Emma were about to finish their course. They'd be returning to the U.K. soon enough. Besides, they were so indifferent. If something was wrong here, obviously, something was wrong with me. My biggest fear.

Between believing I must own everything that happened and my hypervigilant meditation practice, I had no good way of standing up for myself. By the time I articulated my thoughts, I often made situations worse.

"You're right," I nodded at last, though no one was looking at me. "No big deal."

Then along came Polly.

I'm not sure when I became aware of Polly. She appeared on the periphery before showing up in our house. Shortly after the first sighting, however, I saw her everywhere, the beach, outdoor concerts, even the occasional yoga class. Sporting the hippie Ibiza chic very popular at the time—baby halter tops and miniskirts paired with toe booties and belted leather pouches—she also wore a bejeweled bindi between her eyes at all times, even over the breakfast I found myself sharing with her one morning at Hercules Manor's dining table.

"G'morning," Polly said as if this was our regular routine. "You wouldn't happen to have any butter, would you?"

Wondering why this woman was even at our house, I retrieved my non-vegan butter and handed it over. Though I shielded Nicola and Emma from my non-vegetarianism as best I could, I did not pretend to be vegan.

After a few considered strokes with a table knife, Polly looked up again. "Have you got 100 rupees?" she asked. "I need a tuk-tuk back to my place."

Anything to get you out of here faster.

Back at the table with cash in hand, I found Polly slathering Nutella atop her buttered slice, and it all came together. This woman was the weed hookup.

She'd have been welcome everywhere, but especially by Nicola and Emma who, in preparation for their imminent departure, had gone into total debauchery mode. I don't think a single waking hour went by without a joint being lit. I couldn't wait for them to be gone. In the fifteen years since I'd sobered up I'd been around plenty of partying without trouble, but I'd found living with active dope-smokers extremely unpleasant. Once, after riding all the way to Coney Island in Ricky's van while he toked up, I'd explained the torment to Willy. "The smell lingered, but *he* disappeared."

I'd been consoling myself with the knowledge that it would all be over soon. Already I'd been corresponding with the incoming roommate, Jane, a soon-to-be student at Jenny's shala. Mere days before my roommates were scheduled to depart, scary Nicola made an announcement.

"Polly needs a place to stay. She's getting kicked out of her place because she hasn't paid the rent."

Flick, went the lighter. *Gurgle, gurgle*, went the bong.

This didn't sound like anything that concerned me, so I followed the Al-Anon rules and kept my mouth shut.

"It's only a few weeks before she goes back home," Emma chipped in. "We told her she could stay here."

Another flick, more gurgles.

That did concern me. I went straight to nuclear. "Oh, hell no," I said. "That's not going to work."

"Why not?" the girls asked in unison, Emma expelling a cloud of smoke.

"Because I'm not the only one who'll be living here," I said, instantly shucking the blame onto my incoming roommate, Jane. We'd only had a few back and forths, and of course I had no idea how she'd feel about rooming with the local pot dealer, but I was happy to assume.

A writer and a yogi like me, Jane was on the verge of turning thirty. She'd written that she looked forward to having quiet, reflective time in India, away from the hubbub of her life in New Zealand. Even if it turned out we weren't going to be besties, I couldn't wait to share the bathroom with just one person.

"I can't do that to Jane."

"What difference does the new roommate make?" Nicola demanded. "There's more than enough space for a couple of weeks."

"And living here is practically free!" Emma added.

They were both right. Visa travel meant people came and went on schedule. I wouldn't be stuck with Polly forever. As much as I didn't want a freeloading party animal in my space, I worried about appearing priggish. Everyone in Goa partied hard. If word spread that I'd rejected Polly—as opposed to events beyond my control, i.e., Jane—I feared I'd be unwelcome at parties.

Believing I could control what other people thought was a sign that I was still inhabiting the dangerous realm of obsessive-compulsive thinking, a hallmark of my addiction relapse. But even as I saw these foibles, I leaned into self-preservation and held my ground. By blaming someone else.

"I just can't do that to Jane," I repeated.

"You don't know anything about being a yogi," Emma said, thrusting her jaw at me before turning heel and leaving the dining room. Grabbing the bong, Nicola followed. The girl gang was over. Neither spoke to me again, right up to our goodbye, a one-sided conversation where I did all the talking. Had I recreated my marriage dynamic?

"I'm sorry things turned out this way," I said, sounding eerily like an email I'd sent to my ex.

As I shut the door behind them, I wondered. If I'd been on guard enough, maybe I could've hidden my contempt better. But as the smoke cleared the room, rather than tunnel into questions about how I was lacking, I said aloud, "Good riddance, fuckers."

I'd like to think that now I'd be honest but firm. Say something like, "You know I'm way too anal for that. No way."

And then at last, Jane moved in.

"Oh, thank fuck," my new roommate exclaimed in all her Kiwi glory, after she'd arrived at Hercules Manor and I'd confessed. "I would've hated Polly."

"Sorry I made it about you," I said, disarmed by her admission and easy cursing. "I froze."

"Oh please, I would've thrown you under the bus if I had to as well. They knew you hated Polly when they sprang it on you that she should live here."

Except I never said I hated Polly. *Had I?* In my last email to Jane, I mentioned the forehead bling. How she preferred dousing herself in patchouli to showering. How she never had any money. These were just statements of fact. I didn't want Jane getting the idea that I was a judgey twat either.

Between Jane's thick mane of silvery blonde hair, the profusion of blankets and soft fabrics that traveled with her, and the fact that she studied Sivananda-style yoga as opposed to the exercise drill Ashtanga style, I warmed in her presence. Suddenly, all credit to Jane, being myself felt natural.

I laughed.

"Shit. Did I forget to turn off the neon sign over my head?"

"Sign?" Jane shook her head. "With you, love, it's more like a psychic megaphone."

She was right. And so what?

How often had I seen people twitching with rage? They never had to confess their anger. The megaphone did the talking. Not that I should rely upon the reception. Like the Humorous Not-Shrew I'd met at my first vipassana, whose story I'd gotten all wrong.

With Nicola and Emma, I'd been running on apprehension and trying to radiate nonchalance. By dragging my long-held fear into the light without judgment, Jane decommissioned its power in a way that *thinking* about my trauma never had.

Rooming with Jane, even for a short time, was the breakthrough I didn't know I'd been waiting for. I saw how I'd undermined intimacy by not being myself, out of fear that my true self would be poorly received. Knowing how it felt when my speech aligned with my thoughts and feelings was key to knowing when that alignment was off.

"Shall we burn some sage or just stop feeding the cats they left behind?" Jane asked, pulling me from my thoughts.

L.L. Kirchner

"Sage," I said. "Maybe an exorcism."

After speaking with Jane, I went to my room and pulled up a Tara Brach talk in which she described waking up from the "unlived life."

I might have forgotten the talk, but I remembered the story she told, in which a beautiful young woman fell in love with a boy from her village. But the boy was poor, and the girl's father had already promised his daughter to a wealthy man. Upon learning of his beloved's impending nuptials, the young man decided to leave the village. When this news reached the young woman she fell to the floor, unable to speak or move. Her father had to carry her to her room. But the young man snuck to her window to bid farewell, and she jumped out and ran off with him. Even after marrying and having children, they longed for home. Finally, the couple returned to their village to beg for forgiveness.

"You're mistaken," the father said when the young husband tried to apologize. "My daughter hasn't spoken or left the house in five years."

Hearing the commotion, the daughter emerged from inside the house and floated outside. The two figures embraced, and the woman became whole again.

Brach compared this awakening to coming out of a trance. I, too, wanted to break out of this spell.

With every failure to reveal my genuine self, I'd actively created a vaster "unlived" life, leaving parts of myself behind and then wondering why the various versions of me I tried to present failed to attract intimacy.

I'd hidden myself both in intimate relationships and with friends. With everyone I loved.

I did believe the human heart had endless capacity for love. Would I ever find a way to fall in love and stop recreating the dynamic that was no longer serving me? I could start with my friends.

Jane encouraged me to sign up for a restorative yoga workshop. "You will love it," she'd said. "Love." Those were the magic words.

Were it not for Jane's romancing the notion of a softer practice, I doubt I'd ever have taken a restorative course. Little did I know, this would lead me to yet another cult.

HE SAYS IT'S A CULT

Goa, 2013

"Allow yourself to find absolute stillness," cooed our instructor as she lit incense and the woody scent of nag champa drifted across the room, lifting me from the light sleep I'd fallen into.

This was my favorite part of class, savasana. Though I often drifted into sleep, corpse pose isn't meant for napping. The calm inactivity is meant to prepare yogis for the final meditation, death.

"Regard all incoming noise, whether it's chatter in your own mind, a bird, or even the sound of my voice," she went on, "as data. Totally impersonal."

My eyebrows lifted in response to her words. Her words made the challenge sound doable. After class, I stayed behind to help Jacqui stow the myriad bolsters, blocks, and blankets we used during class. I was also curious.

"What you were saying about data struck a real chord. Though I'm not great at *not* taking things personally. A mosquito can bite me, and I'll think, 'What did I do to you?'"

Jacqui laughed. "Oh, me too, but with some help, I'm learning how to quit doing that."

Jacqui felt that way, too?

I considered my teacher. Between her Lululemon gear and brunette bob squared to her jawline, she put off a decidedly less boho vibe than other yogis I'd met in India, but she radiated a serene glow nonetheless. She and her partner, David, had built this treehouse retreat with ecotourists and contemporary design in mind—the platform where we'd just practiced was open on all sides and offered a stunning view from within the canopy. I was lucky to have secured a spot; typically their retreats were booked solid.

"What do you mean *learning* to quit? Are you taking a class?"

"Well, I go to these meetings," she said.

"Like 12-Step meetings?" I asked, hopeful. Though I'd been to meetings in India, I'd never heard anything like that. Maybe she'd take me to some groovy new meeting.

"No, not like that. Well, actually, I don't know. I've never been to one." She looked at the ground as if embarrassed. "It's more like a class."

She told me that the lectures were offered in the next town over, Arambol.

"But David won't go. He calls the place a cult." Jacqui smiled, looked at the ground, then back at me. "Of course, it isn't."

Just then, I saw David behind her, his dark mane of curly waves undulating as he stomped across the grounds, an air of impatience following him. I wanted Jacqui's poise and tranquility, not David's restless edginess.

What do I have to lose?

"I'd love to come with you sometime," I said.

"I'm heading there now," she said. "Come."

In the tuk-tuk on the way to Arambol, Jacqui opened up.

"I'm feeling really conflicted," she said. "David's so against Balanced View that he doesn't want me to go at all. He's even threatened to leave."

Her candor astounded me. I wanted to know every detail, but my questions felt too invasive. She didn't need my armchair opinion on her relationship, but I was curious. "Balanced View?"

"That's the name of the group. They have several locations. The Arambol center is one."

When I thought of cults, I didn't think of branch campuses. What came to mind were communal societies whose leaders took out their residents in stunning fashion, literally and figuratively as they tended to dress oddly. Woefully incomplete as my understanding was, I wasn't altogether wrong.

Whether the place was a cult or not, I was unafraid. I'd just stayed at one, Osho, and gleaned valuable lessons. Because no matter what turns they took, cults always started off around a good idea. Even adding the economic exploitation and obsession with attracting new members to the definition, you could use the word cult to describe the Girl Scouts. I always liked being a Girl Scout. I couldn't wait to check out Balanced View.

The center's grounds were separated from the main drag by a parking lot and a long dirt footpath. As we walked between tall palms, the outbuildings came into view—cement block structures painted in bright yellows. Billowing silk tapestries provided shade and created an effect somewhere between humble ashram and groovy meditation resort.

Jacqui picked up the pace as we neared the lecture hall, passing fragrant rows of frangipani and signs pointing to offices, classrooms, and living quarters. We arrived to find the session had already begun.

The assembly area was similar to Jenny's shala, a cement pad topped by a thatched roof. Rows of white plastic chairs faced a podium on a raised platform that was adorned with pink and white wildflowers. There had to be more than a hundred people in the audience.

"You learn to tap into open intelligence," the teacher was saying, as we spotted two chairs together in a row toward the back. "This open intelligence is inexhaustible."

Scanning the crowd as we squeezed between the patchouli-scented audience members, I found not an Indian in sight. *Is this something only the tourists can afford?* I wondered. *Or do the locals just know better?* I tried to catch Jacqui's eye as we took our seats, but she was staring ahead, riveted already.

"Allow yourself to be exactly as you are and sense what you feel when thought is not present," the woman up front said in lilting Israeli tones. "Close your eyes and stop thinking, for just the briefest moment." Then she went still, eyes shut.

She meant now?

In a split-second calculation, I reasoned that compared to other attempts I'd made at spiritual healing, like sitting silently for hours at a time, chanting complex mantras, or finding a vaguely orgiastic circle to join at a sex ashram, letting go of thought for a moment was easily doable.

Closing my eyes, I shut off my brain. The rat-a-tat of a kingfisher's song pulled me back. This cessation couldn't have lasted more than a second or two, but even in that short time, I felt it—my Inner Buddha. Without stories or pain or effort on top of it, at my core was an undeniable feeling of optimism. Relief surged through me—*I* do *have an Inner Buddha. And that bitch is blissed out!*

Everything that got in the way of connecting with that being, I understood at once, was what I piled on. In the same way my perceptions clouded everything I saw in the exterior world, I'd directed a similarly false lens at the interior.

"We recognize alertness and stability. Clarity," the teacher said. "The power to know. Open intelligence."

Her only instruction was to keep doing this practice as the idea occurred to us. "Whether it's once a day or once a week, it's fine. You start where you are, taking short moments, and see what happens."

Whenever? Wherever?

"In the next moment, when thoughts and emotions come, we call it all data."

The teacher leaned forward at the podium. "But that open intelligence, it doesn't go anywhere. Over time we see that data is inseparable from open intelligence.

"Whenever data arises, we relax body and mind and rely on the power of open intelligence. What a comfort to know. I don't need to change anything about myself, my thoughts, or feelings."

Didn't need to change anything? Wait. Had I been going about this entire search wrong?

For the duration of my spiritual search, I'd been fixated on detecting my faults. The idea that I didn't need to change anything about myself was a revolution. Chasing down my flaws had proven to be an endlessly unsatisfiable hunt. There would always be something to find. Maybe I should look for my own "secret beauty." What if, instead of foraging for my character defects, I started actively noticing my character assets?

I went back to Balanced View the next day, without Jacqui.

Candice O'Denver, the leader of Balanced View, kicked off the session from Sweden via videoconference.

"The mind is a point of view just like any other," she said in a vaguely mid-Atlantic cadence. "No matter how we define that point of view, it's not the same as reality. Yet all points of view are valid. So how do we know what is real?"

I straightened my spine, on the edge of my seat.

"Awareness."

She went on to describe how accessing "open intelligence" was a tool for developing this perception. I knew it was a sales pitch, but this was where she got me.

After describing the many master teachers she'd studied with over the years, O'Denver had concluded there was too much dogma and hierarchy in spiritual practice. These systems got in the way of the open intelligence available to us all.

Had these layers of, essentially, bureaucracy been in my way?

Whether it was the poses given only to advanced Ashtanga yoga students, the rigid structure of Nichiren, or the tantric knowledge held by Osho's sannyasins alone, the layering imposed a distance between people and all things sacred in much the same way Catholicism had. Resentful as I was about these hierarchies, I gravitated toward them if I didn't examine my beliefs more deeply.

Back in teacher training, when our yoga philosophy teacher had presented Patanjali's dualistic beliefs as something outmoded—having been replaced by the notion of Oneness—I'd agreed with the ancient yogi. Of course the gods were external to sentient beings. Seeing the divine as something outside myself had been reinforced in 12-Step recovery too. "To have faith all you need to know is that there's a god and you ain't it," was a saying often touted. But now, sitting there in that lecture hall listening to Candice O'Denver, I felt ready to accept my divine nature.

Taking a deep breath to clear the truth bombing

moment, I looked around the room. The woman who'd given yesterday's lecture, Inbal, was seated in the audience with the rest of us. Now, a student herself. I liked that.

"Open intelligence can erase the experience of data," O'Denver said. "Say you've had an issue with abandonment. You've tried everything, bought a hundred self-help books, gone to trainings, therapy. But still, the fear lingers. With open intelligence, the anguish and torment vanishes."

When her lecture ended, I signed up for the introductory course, Basic Awareness.

Class began a few days later, co-led by Inbal, from the first lecture, and Adrian, a tattooed Brit who struck me as a former addict of some kind, not that he ever said so. I liked them both immensely. What I found groundbreaking about Balanced View's approach was its insistence on the accessibility of open intelligence. Though I didn't need Balanced View to connect with open intelligence, I started wondering how I might stay in contact with the group, but they didn't have a center in New York City. *Maybe I'd start one.*

Over a saffron-infused rice and veg curry at Balanced View's outdoor café, I looked around at the community. Spread out over blankets was a mass of tie-dye and leather outerwear, in some ways more uniform than most Catholic high school standards. Jacqui's boyfriend was right, this place was a cult.

In her book, *Cultish*—which came out years after my

brush with Balanced View—Amanda Montell describes a cult as any group that separates itself from outsiders by its language. By her definition, what may have saved me from getting sucked in to many cultish groups I interacted with, was the love of words my mom instilled from an early age, including a balanced view. Much as O'Denver's teachings resonated, I didn't see myself cozying up to Data any more than I had to Truth. Between my yoga, meditation, and 12-Step groups, I was in enough cults already. And I could tune into open intelligence on my own.

MR. RIGHT

Goa, 2013

I was on my balcony typing away when I heard the text notification come in. *Ding, ding.*

Looking down at my phone I saw Hugh's name. I tapped the new message.

```
Surprise    darling!    M    on    way    2
Anjuna!!
```

And he was where? *Ding, ding.*

```
Will be at yours for dinner!
```

That was in just a few hours' time. Rather than text back immediately with something along the lines of, "Are you out of your mind to show up unannounced?" I took a short moment. Since Balanced View I'd begun doing this practice regularly, and to great effect.

Just that morning I'd tried it out with a shopkeeper. My flip-flop had torn on a stairstep, necessitating immediate replacement. I found a pair of brown rubber thongs that should've cost around eighty-five rupees. When I took the sandals to the shopkeeper, however, he smiled broadly and said, straight-faced, "Five hundred rupees." Bargaining was expected but a ritual I disliked. I didn't enjoy haggling. What if I asked for open intelligence?

In what barely registered as a beat in the conversation, I dropped all thought and felt for the joyful self within. Without strategizing I simply smiled back and asked, "But what's your friendliest price?"

Minor though the triumph was, our negotiation went smoothly, and I left with my new rubber thongs at the price I knew they should be. Not only was this practice easier than the drudgery of sitting still for long periods of time, but the effects had been far more tangible.

When it came to responding to Hugh, however, no such answer came. I didn't want him to stay the night, much less for an extended period. But given how our previous joint living arrangement had begun, it wasn't so unreasonable for him to assume I wouldn't mind if he showed up unannounced.

I lifted my head from my phone. Was that cinnamon and warm milk I smelled wafting up the stairs? Jane must be back from yoga and making masala chai. What would she do?

"Maybe it'll be nice to see him," she said when I showed her the message on my Nokia burner. "Would you like a chai?"

"Yes please." I grabbed a mug from its hook, keeping an eye on Jane's face as she stirred. "But what the hell? This is how he tells me he's coming?"

Maintaining a serene look on her face, Jane shut off the cooktop and poured our drinks. To give her space to maneuver I had to back into the dining room, where she joined me at the table.

"It is bizarre him telling you he's coming while he's on the way, but didn't you say you thought you might be building something with him?"

I nodded, inhaling the spicy scent rising from my mug before taking a sip. "This chai is delicious."

Jane sat and took a drink, murmuring in agreement before asking, "Didn't you say you thought you two might be building something in Osho? He could be just passing through. Or maybe he has somewhere else to stay."

True, Hugh hadn't said anything about staying. And I didn't want to be the one, as Svagito would've said, "doing the rejecting." Rather, I wanted to embrace the "what isness" as Sambhavo had taught. "You're right. What's the worst that could happen?"

I wrote Hugh.

`C u soon! How long will u be here?`

My way of not asking directly if he planned to stay.

This was the final layer of dishonesty I needed to eliminate: *self*-deception. My aspiration to be a laid-back person who could hang with uncertainty ignored the fact I was my mother's daughter, adept at finding the black cloud in the silver lining. And though it remains my least favorite aspect, there's a difference between discouraging a trait and pretending it doesn't exist. Wanting to be okay with something I was not okay with never worked. For the first time in my travels, I longed to be back in New

270

York City. After scrambling around in the "why" of my unhappiness, I'd changed everything and remained dissatisfied. But blaming myself did no good. Better to find something to love and appreciate. I could do that just as well at home.

"Hello, darling," Hugh said, dropping his bag to hug me. Speaking into my hair, he said he'd just seen my text. "I'm not sure what my plans are."

He smiled so I tried to smile back, find the warmth in his gray eyes, invoke the desire to touch his gray beard, but no. This was the first time I'd seen Hugh in something other than maroon robes and it caused neither my masculine nor feminine aspects to rise. My heart definitely sank. I hoped he might have an alternative to the flowy black pants and collarless shirt in his satchel, but no, Applebee's host was pretty much his look.

"Are you... do you have a plan?" I couldn't bring myself to ask. It hadn't been all that long since he'd welcomed me into his place with open arms.

"I just thought I'd come and get a feel for Goa."

When we left for dinner however, he also left behind his bag. Obviously he felt he was staying.

Over a meal of fresh fish curry, Hugh told me about the three-week meditation course he'd taken at Osho and his subsequent travels. While he talked, I tried to rekindle the spark. When his words failed to move me, I tried moving on to his finer points, his tidy beard and nails. His straight and narrow nose. His stone-colored eyes. What had happened to the attraction? My feelings for Hugh had changed just like that hair in Goenka's soup; they'd been about context.

Hugh was still talking. "I'm just vibing on co-creating with all this beautiful energy in India."

After dinner, we went home and shagged. The encounter wasn't terrible, but the thrill had vanished. By the next morning, Hugh was on my last nerve.

Over an oatmeal breakfast, Hugh expressed the desire to spend the day cavorting at the beach. Already at a deficit—I'd failed to set my alarm the night before and missed yoga—I wanted to spend the day far away from Hugh. When I reached for open intelligence, those Al-Anon tenets came to mind: Does it need to be said? Does it need to be said right now? Does it need to be said by me?

Hugh did not need to hear how I yearned to escape, but I could still be truthful. "I need to get to the internet café and post office."

"Wouldn't you rather partake of Leela?"

He was talking about the spirit of play at the center of the universe, a notion we'd discussed at Osho. Our ashram experience had been all about staring into each other's eyes and making earnest observations. And though I'd been guilty of taking that ambience into the real world myself, I liked to think I knew when to quit. Hugh suffered no such censor.

"Is it because you were sunburned so badly as a child that you went to hospital?"

Gimme a break, I thought, another utterance Al-Anon reasoned did not need to be said. "I don't think so. I never go to the beach during prime tanning hours."

"Your mother can't hurt you here!"

Now there was a leap, but again I had nothing to say.

"I believe in you. Maybe you can't have children, but you can be mother to yourself."

Step back, jagoff. You're the one here who wants a mommy to indulge you.

That thought, I was sure, should only be said by Hugh's therapist. But Hugh read my silence as acquiescence to his wisdom.

"Come. Sit with me. Let's close our eyes and touch in with goddess energy."

We were seconds away from a chakra healing. Something had to be said, and right now, I was going to have to be the one to say it.

"Hugh, we slept in, and I have to get to the internet café before it closes for lunch."

"We need to talk about your avoidance."

Fuck. There's pretty much no way to get out of talking about avoidant behavior without coming across as, at the very least, evasive. Short of him leaving, I wanted nothing more than to escape. Of course I didn't need to go to the internet café.

"Sorry, I have to go. We can talk later."

"I don't even want to fuck him anymore," I stage-whispered to Jane in the bathroom that night while she brushed her teeth. "Everything about him is getting on my tits, his beard, the sound of his voice, the words that come out."

She spit into the sink. "Tell him to leave."

Well, I couldn't. But if Jane asked me to ask him, I could totally kick him out. "Do you want him out?"

"I don't mind if he stays," she said.

Damnit.

The next night, I hauled Hugh on the back of my scooter to a concert in Vagator, the next town over. Anxious to get around anyone who wasn't Hugh, I practically ran for the section of the beach where the musicians were playing.

The show blew me away. A twenty-something man sang traditional Israeli folk songs while alternating between a traditional lute-type instrument (which I later learned was called an oud) and a flute. His bandmates were an Australian on didgeridoo, an Indian with a tabla, and an African on bongo drums.

"I love when he translates the lyrics," I said to Hugh.

"It's just good to see you happy," he said.

I scowled. Could we not have one moment in sync rather than in scrutiny?

The concert ended. As we traipsed through the dark sea of two-wheelers in search of my scooter, Hugh wanted to talk some more.

"I can't find the bike with you talking," I said. "Do you mind?"

"You don't know where your bike is?"

In my rush to get off the scooter and be around anyone that wasn't Hugh, I'd not committed the parking spot to memory. Everyone in Goa rides either a scooter or a motorcycle, and the space was unlit.

"Do *you*?"

"I think," he said. "It's this way."

I walked with him, but my instinct told me to walk in the opposite direction. I couldn't ignore my gut another moment.

"I don't think it's this way," I said and pivoted.

"No," he said. "It's this way."

You don't know but of course you think you're more right than me. You arrogant fuck.

"We can split up," I told him. "Or we can look together, but I have the keys, and I don't want to have to find you."

As we searched for my scooter, I was pretty sure my hint that I'd leave him behind had not come from a place of open intelligence or love. When enough people cleared, we found my scooter. As it turned out, Hugh was right. Or more right than I'd been about the bike's general direction.

"You were right," I said, wanting to offer something. "Let's go home."

"You're incredible. Absolutely incredible," he said, clearly referring to *my* arrogance.

He wasn't wrong, but I was tired. I hopped onto my Honda and patted the seat behind me. "Get on." Again, I didn't say it, but the implication was there. I was leaving with or without him.

"I will *not* get on," Hugh said, crossing his arms without moving from the gravel lot. "We need to talk."

I could not have disagreed more.

In response, I put the keys in the ignition and turned the engine. Hugh scrambled aboard, then spent the entire ride home yelling at me from the back of the scooter. Background noise. Data. Totally impersonal.

The feeling of strength I felt as he unraveled and I observed was extraordinary. Back at Hercules Manor we went straight to bed, fully dressed. He was gone when I woke up.

"Hurrah!" I squealed to Jane over our shared breakfast of toast and mangoes. We often ate together. Unlike my previous roommates, I never felt judged by Jane, though she, too, was a vegetarian.

"God, if you knew it was going to be that easy, you could've gotten rid of him so much faster."

"I thought the fact we only had sex the first night would do it," I said, buttering a slice of Portuguese bread.

"The weird thing was, there was *nothing* Hugh could've done or said on that bike to get me to fight with him. He was out of his *mind,* and I did not give one fuck. I enjoyed watching him twist in the wind."

So what if I was essentially talking through my deep feelings with Jane? I wanted to hear what she had to say. A breakup had spurred her trip to India as well, so, like me, she was versed in therapy-speak.

"But this is the wildest part, at some point during his rant, I realized I'd done the same dance with my ex. Only this time, Hugh was playing me, while I took the role of my ex-husband." I shook my head, flabbergasted at how good this realization felt. "That's when I knew, there was nothing I could have done differently to *save* my marriage."

Jane dipped a chunk of mango into her yogurt. "That's the irony, isn't it? In passive-aggressive dynamics, it's the passive one who's in control."

"How have I never heard that before?" I asked,

though I knew I probably had, only I'd never been ready to hear it before.

"I dare say it takes two people," Jane said. "We can all fall into these patterns. Unless you're really toxic, it's not that one person is right and the other wrong. It's, what do we bring out in each other?"

From my balcony perch later that day, after yoga, I recalled a conversation with my former spouse. "People don't change," he'd said not long after we first met when I asked if he'd ever been in therapy.

Having spent more than a decade around recovering addicts already, I couldn't have disagreed more. I'd seen people change dramatically on a regular basis. But did I disagree? No, I rationalized. *My sweetheart is so healthy he doesn't need therapy.*

Recalling this now, I smiled at what an innocent I'd been, and felt no need to get stuck in that rabbit hole. I might've turned my search for absolution into another addiction, but that meant recovery was also possible.

"Jane!" I called downstairs. "Wanna go to the Wednesday market?"

HOLY SHIT, I'M AN AUTHOR

New York City, 2013

"You'll never believe this," I gushed to Willy over a plate of noodles at the East Village's Tai Thai, a few months after I'd returned from my extended departure. I'd found another apartment in our Alphabet City neighborhood.

He looked up at me over his dish, eyes hooded.

"I think I finally let it go!" I was so pleased with myself.

"Let me guess," he said, dropping his chopsticks. "This is about your ex-husband."

I looked into my lap. Was Willy annoyed I'd stopped accompanying him to his chanting group?

"It is, but I swear this breakthrough is big. And I realized it because of storytelling."

278

New York had a rich storytelling scene. Though I still took writing classes as often as I could, getting up and telling audiences about my experiences in Qatar offered more editorial guidance. A crowd let you know right away when your material didn't work.

"You know how I've worried that telling stories might be a problem, actually causing me to reactivate the old patterns I had with my ex?"

He looked at me, still quiet.

"That storytelling brain, though, is much bigger than those crafted tales. Even when I've tried praying for my ex to get rid of resentments, like they say to do in the program, I couldn't do it without *some* backstory starting. So, recently, I figured I'd try praying for my ex like taking a short moment. Drop all the narrative and picture him happy. Just his face, laughing. Nothing else, no commentary whatsoever. The practice has done wonders. The despondency I used to feel around that whole situation? Gone. I only wish him the best."

He signaled for the waitress. "Can we get the check?"

Later that day, I texted him.

Wanna hit the beach this weekend?

No response. I tried calling. "Hey Willy, it's me. Call me back."

Nothing.

His silence set off a keening in my heart. We went from speaking multiple times a day and meeting several times a week to having no contact. I went by his place to be sure he was all right.

When Willy didn't answer, I knew. Maybe he was home. Maybe he wasn't. Either way, he'd quit me.

The withdrawal was an echo of my divorce, but with one key difference. This time I knew what I'd done. I'd turned our relationship into exactly what he'd feared from the outset, "one of those one-way deals where it's all just you dumping your shit."

Not that understanding felt better. While ultimately, this breakup would give me another chance to grow a bigger and more sparkly Higher Power, in the interim I was hurt, but didn't try to deny the pain.

Turning away from Willy's buzzer, I remembered another of Ram Dass' stories, about a letter he'd sent to parents suffering the loss of a child.

"If you close your heart down to anything in the universe... you are then at the mercy of suffering. To have finally dealt with suffering, you have to consume it into yourself... and be able to keep your heart open in hell."

Before I reached my building my phone rang. It was my editor.

My editor.

When my first agent gave up trying to sell my book, I'd written a one-woman show based on the story. Coming at the material from this new perspective had led to making a deal with a small press to publish my memoir. "Holy shit, Mom," I'd enthused into the phone. "I'm going to be an author."

"I'm not surprised," she'd said, mysteriously. "But you know I don't like it when you swear."

I looked at the time. *Shit.* We were supposed to be

going through some manuscript edits. "Let me call you back as soon as I'm at my computer. Sorry!"

My beloved Hartley greeted me at the door.

A punchline I'd thrown into many of my stories was that I missed my dogs more than I missed my husband. But it was no joke.

Shortly after returning from India, all that changed over brunch with a friend. "Look at that," Paola had said, pointing through the diner's window. "Badass Brooklyn Animal Rescue is hosting an event."

Following her finger, I saw a stream of people who—despite the bitter cold—were walking around the block with dogs sporting neon vests that beckoned, "Adopt Me!"

"Let's go check it out," I said, and will be forever grateful Paola agreed.

At the event we were directed to wait inside until one of the dogs became available. "What about him?" I asked, pointing to a sweet little chestnut-colored pup shivering in the corner.

"Oh, yeah. Hal doesn't seem to like the cold."

After my heart!

I knelt down and he immediately walked over and threw his paws around my neck.

"Him," I said. "I'll take him."

Being a New York City rescue operation, the adoption process was rigorous. Even with a recommendation from one of the adoption agency's board members, I had to face a home inspection. What if I didn't get him? There had to be scads of applicants vying for those two feet of solid muscle, flying nun ears, and amber eyes.

When the volunteer came to inspect my apartment, I showed her around my studio and bragged about my proximity to Tompkins Square Park. Then the unthinkable happened. She unhooked his leash. "We're not supposed to leave the dogs on the first visit. But I can tell, you're ready for Hal Hartley."

And she was gone. "Hartley!" I was keeping that part of the indie film director's name. "Let's go for a walk!"

Kneeling now to rub Hartley's chest, I felt more grateful than ever for the outward bound, unconditional love he'd brought into my life. Hartley wasn't trying to pee in the wrong place or destroy my underwear or dismantle my garbage can. All I ever saw was his secret beauty. But I needed to call my editor back.

When I pulled my hand away, Hartley laid his paw on my forearm. He wasn't done enjoying the scratch. Not that he or the book deal could replace Willy, but if Hartley had taught me anything, it was the value of being in the present moment. I didn't need to leave claw marks on everything I let go of.

When the Qatar book came out about a year after my return to the States, I put together an ambitious book tour to promote it, which included buying a car. The Bianchi road bike remained my primary mode of transportation, but the old Jetta enabled me to take Hartley everywhere.

Somewhere toward the middle of that tour—more precisely, a friends' couch-surfing tour—I found myself driving in circles on Columbus' I-270, shallow-breathed. I kept missing the exit. If I didn't cut it out, I was going to miss the yoga workshop I was supposed to be teaching.

Ding, ding.

I shouldn't have but of course I looked.

`Am in ER. Love, Mom.`

By this time my mother had been living with Stage IV lung and lymph cancer for seven years. My friend Andy, a science journalist, had given me reassuring pep talks about the new paradigm for cancer patients. "We don't talk about having cancer, which sounds like a death sentence, but living with cancer." So, though I hadn't forgotten about her diagnosis, it had receded in prominence. This text felt different, though there was no logic to why.

Over the years my mother had developed a real fondness for texting from doctors' offices and hospitals and even ERs. I don't know what tickled me more, her zest for learning new technology at seventy-three or the fact that she included an identifier on her texts. But this note didn't put a smile on my face. I called immediately.

"Hey Mom, just trying to give you a call back. You probably can't talk since you're in the ER, but if you get a chance call me back. I'll be offline for a couple hours teaching, but you can leave a message. What happened?"

The studio was on the second floor of a building that had housed a thrift shop back when I'd been a student at Ohio State. If I didn't know I was in Columbus, I'd never have guessed. The metamorphosis was dramatic.

By the time I padded into the room, the students were grumbling.

"I am so sorry I'm late. I thought I knew just how to get here but I was wrong. If I were in your place, I'd be pissed, too. Which is a great place to start. Let's begin."

The yoga workshop I'd devised to help pay for my book tour didn't have much to do with my book, but it made a huge media splash. And while I sold my memoir at the workshops, the class itself was more a testament to the experiences that inform this book—a combination of meditation and movement, inspired by a meditation teacher I met in India, Robert, who told me he'd been doing vipassana meditation for thirty years.

"Does meditating ever get any easier?" I asked.

He looked at me and smiled, his gaze a warm embrace. "When I first started meditating, my mind was like a neglected old attic, full of cobwebs and boxes," he said. "After 30 years of meditating, it's all still there, there's just more room between the boxes."

Once I accepted I wasn't going to meditate my way into bliss, I started looking into the mind-body connection. My explorations uncovered two unrelated facts. The first was that, during yoga practice I regularly experienced deep emotions burbling to the surface. Second, I uncovered research showing that trauma gets stored in the pre-verbal, lizard part of the brain. I'd never be able to think or talk away my deepest hurts—I might never eliminate my internal barriers at all—but I could make room for them.

I started making note of the emotions brought up by various postures and practiced specific sequences in an attempt to allow and release deep traumas. This practice became the basis of *Yoga for Getting Over It.*

Not-so-secretly, I was thrilled that being late for this workshop had thus far been the only hiccup of the tour. As often happened, I lost myself in teaching. Then the session was over, and I remembered. *Mom.*

I had to go to Pittsburgh.

Or did I? Was I being dramatic? My mother had been fending off death despite a Stage IV cancer diagnosis for seven goddamn years.

For two weeks, I vacillated. I knew how to leave—I could find subs for my classes and get someone into my apartment—but I didn't want to. Was I trying to help her, or sabotage myself? Nobody leaves the publishing capital of the world just as their book launches.

Yet I couldn't shake the hunch the end was near. I should go to my mother's side,

Another sticking point was where I would stay. I loved my family but when I stayed with them, I reverted. Or maybe we had that effect on each other. Regardless, that was not the energy I wanted to take to the readings and yoga workshops I still had on my schedule.

There was some comfort in this ambivalence—it thrust another recovery dictum into perspective. For years I'd used the slogan, "pain is the touchstone of spiritual growth," as encouragement to seek out needless difficulty.

But was this "needless"?

My tenants in Pittsburgh called. They were so sorry, but something had come up. They had to vacate their lease early. Was it a problem?

That put an end to my questions.

DEEP BREATH

Murrysville, 2014

I'd been in Pittsburgh about six weeks when it happened. During Mom's insomniac wanderings one night, she bumped into Dad's piano bench, fell, and snapped her collarbone. It hadn't been all that long since she'd had a port to her kidney installed. After seven years of toxic infusions, her body was in revolt.

"Your goddamned father can't even push in his own goddamned chair," Mom growled from her hospital bed just before her face lit up. "Bob!"

My father had just arrived at the hospital, joining my sister and me after having been summoned to meet with Mom's doctor.

Up till now, we'd all followed our somewhat normal routines. Dad went to and from work at the gym while Mom stayed home and went on a cleaning tear. I picked up some yoga teaching gigs and even started a storytelling show at a little coffee shop near my duplex. My sister Tess, who'd moved back to Pittsburgh, regularly posted Mom's progress—both in cleaning and healing—on social media. Mom hadn't even lost her hair.

Chemo really has advanced, I thought, wondering if I should go back to New York though soon I'd learn that hair loss resulted from radiation therapy, a treatment that had been suspended for my mother.

"Nobody thinks I'm a patient," Mom said. "They come in the room and ask, 'Where's Mary?' I just don't look like somebody with cancer!"

She wasn't wrong. Later I'd think there was a cruelty in her healthful appearance.

We continued the casual banter around her hospital bed until the doctor arrived.

"It's time for hospice," he said as my dad, Tess, and I stood wide-eyed around the bed. "Time to stop medical care."

No more care like she's in remission and it's not needed or like hospice she's dying? Can't people be in hospice for years?

These questions went unanswered, probably because they went unasked.

"We'll be discharging her tomorrow morning," the doctor said, and then left the room, a cursory appearance that failed to register either his name or his face in my memory.

Perhaps he assumed that, given the length of Mom's illness, we'd discussed what to do in such an event. We had not.

Regardless of his prognosis, starting the next day,

Mom was going to need round-the-clock care. Actively dying or not, between the port and her broken collarbone, she couldn't get herself to the bathroom or flip herself around. Lying on her back was extremely uncomfortable, as was resting on either her left or right side.

"I've got to be at the gym tomorrow morning," Dad said.

None of us spoke.

Tess had just started at a new job; she'd snuck out on a long lunch for this chat. I was scheduled to leave that very afternoon to speak at a college, a paying gig I could not afford to cancel. Relatively speaking, Dad being at the gym was the least pressing engagement. Though the membership roster had dwindled in recent years, he still had employees. Why not bring in one of the paid staff to work the reception desk? Hell, maybe close the place for a few hours. Family emergency and all that. If he couldn't be bothered to see Mom safely out of the hospital, how was he planning to take care of her once she got home?

This is how he copes, I reminded myself, taking a deep breath.

Somehow, we left that room without resolving anything as if the next steps would resolve themselves. I hit the road, Tess returned to work, and Dad went back to the gym.

Convinced I was more right than anyone else, I took a short moment. *Call the hospital back.*

As I drove out of town, I called the hospital to ask about my options. They sent me to a nursing home, where they suggested reaching out to Mom's insurer, where the phone chain stopped. They wouldn't cover a stay at a hospital, a nursing home, or for an in-home nurse. *Wasn't Medicare supposed to be better than this?*

I was considering turning back when the assisted living facility nearest my parents' house called me back. "You say she has a broken collarbone?" the nurse asked, not stopping to wait for an answer. "We can admit her for physical therapy. Medicare will cover that cost for ten days."

Plenty of time to find in-home healthcare. "Thank you," I said. *For finding that loophole.*

While pumping gas into my Jetta, I called Dad with the good news.

"What, do you want her in the ground now?" he yelled.

As surely as if he'd struck me with his palm, I felt stung and reacted as such. "Dad, Mom can't be at home by herself," I said, my words reflecting all the sympathy I could muster, which was none. "How were *you* planning on getting her home? Uber?"

He hung up.

The stink of petrol mixed with the prick of his words. Nonetheless, as the miles to West Virginia ticked by, I replayed the afternoon's details. I couldn't imagine doing anything differently.

On my return the following day, my sister reported that Mom had been transported to the assisted living facility by ambulance. By the time I reached the nursing home later that afternoon, her speech was garbled. She kept falling asleep.

As nursing homes went the facility seemed nice enough, appointed with homey décor, a beauty salon, and regular entertainment. The place was also refreshingly free of that urine-tinged disinfectant scent that pervades so many healthcare facilities. And, as I now know, patients often respond to being moved with a steep cognitive decline. Nonetheless, my first instinct was to react as if they'd done something wrong.

"How much medication is she on?" I demanded at the nurse's station, wondering if they'd lulled her into passivity with chemical restraints.

But as the days wore on and she communicated less, I could no longer deny the real issue. The cancer was metastasizing rapidly.

Before the tenth day elapsed, the evening came when staff brought in a rolling cart packed with coffee and pastries. "I'll take the overnight vigil," I told my dad and sister.

"Your dad spent most of his visiting hours at the nurses' station," one of the nurses told me, shaking her head as she leaned to reach my mom's morphine drip. "He said he was going to get her on a vegan diet when she gets out of here."

"That *would* kill her."

Later, when the hospice nurse arrived, I regaled her with stories about my mother. A force of nature. "She was voted 'Class Wit' in high school," I said. "She's still the funniest person I know. And so chic. Even in high school, I could never fit into her Chanel-style suits." Moments I hadn't thought about in years surfaced.

"She used to buy the three of us matching outfits.

Usually for holidays, but one time she got my sister and me matching maxi-coats." Seeing the nurse's furrowed brow I explained, "Coats that reach your shins? Anyway, they were blue faux fur with white trim and metal clasps that ran down the front. The priest ended up giving a homily about how women should dress modestly. Mom was like, 'He knows how to guilt out the donations.'"

The stories were still going strong when Hartley jumped onto Mom's bed for the first time ever, calling attention to the slowing of her choppy breath. As she exhaled her last, my mother looked at me and for a moment there was a knowing clarity in her face. The gold flecks in her deep brown eyes shone and a burst of stars rained over me. Unconditional. Everlasting. Bigger and more sparkly than I'd ever let myself know.

Love.

EPILOGUE

Pennsylvania-Florida, 2015

I knelt in the clammy basement with a box cutter, feeling as if I might throw up. Ten years of dust and mold were getting to me, but not nearly so much as the contents of the cardboard boxes I was pawing through.

Barely six months had elapsed since Mom's text—*Am in ER. Love, Mom.*—and here I was, preparing to leave my duplex behind forever.

In the face of her death, I had not been yogic and stoic. There was nothing imaginary about this line. I was at yet another precipice. The edge was clear and I knew what I felt—grief comes when love has nowhere to land. My touchstone was gone, but I no longer felt adrift. I let it break me.

That December had been one of the coldest on record in Pittsburgh. For as long as my breath was visible in the draftier corners of my duplex, I cleaned and cleared and

292

readied the space for tenants, eager for spring in New York City. When I wasn't digging through boxes, I taught classes, ran my show at the coffee shop, and walked Hartley. When the time came to leave, for once, I wanted to be ready.

Though my agenda had changed somewhat, I was still in no particular hurry that afternoon when I heard my cell phone ring. Right away I sheathed my utility knife, wiped my hands on my jeans, and threaded through the boxes to where my mobile buzzed on a chest of drawers I needed to get rid of. *Tess.*

"You're moving to Florida?" my sister asked.

"I'm not *moving* there," I said. "But when I was there last fall for my book, Uncle Tommy showed me condos that were only $70,000. I figure I can buy something there, and it'll be at least as rentable as this place."

The truth was somewhat more complicated.

The unit in my "charming" duplex quickly attracted potential tenants. While showing the first applicant around, I tried to get ahead of expectations by explaining the unit's quirks. "You have to sit sideways on the toilet, otherwise your knees slam into the tub." At the end of our tour, he offered to buy the whole house.

But my duplex wasn't for sale. Renting the place had enabled me to survive as a freelancer and travel the globe, offering the constancy of predictable income. Yet I wanted to offer a friendly refusal, so I took a short moment. My mother's voice launched into my head, naming an outrageous amount. "Take that if he offers," she insisted. *Yeah, right*, I thought at her.

Perhaps sensing I was about to turn him down, my

prospect named an amount that would allow me to pay off the mortgage and leave enough to buy a condo in Florida. The exact price my mother had just named. In my head.

"I'm not going to *live* in Florida permanently," I told my sister. "But I can't rent out the condo there till I've owned it for a year. And anyway, I already have someone in my New York apartment, so this'll be a great opportunity to write."

When we got off the phone I hoped I sounded surer than I felt. *Who leaves New York City for their* writing *career? Unless it's for L.A. Should I move to L.A.?* Then I looked back into the box I'd just slit open. A jumble of socks, a tiny brass bear twirling a jade ball, and some family photos, all of which belonged to my ex.

"Cut it out with those boxes," I heard my mom say. "You haven't looked at this crap in ten years. What do you think you're going to find?"

This was wildly unlike the Mom of recent years, a woman who'd become loath to throw anything away, though the voice was unmistakably hers. Wasn't it? Or was the edict more like something I'd say? Did it matter? These cartons had been delivered here from Qatar ten years prior. Were those claw marks I saw?

I called my sister back. "Wanna have a little fun?"

"Always."

I picked her up and off we went, seeking out open dumpsters and tossing in the unopened boxes, laughing the entire time. Even later, when I realized I'd thrown away years' worth of Christmas decorations my mother and I had collected together, I wouldn't have changed a thing about the afternoon. Moving forward was more important than holding on to a life that no longer served me.

En route to the new condo, I realized I'd be driving past Cassadaga, the so-called psychic capital of the world. Another near miss of a story I pitched long ago, Cassadaga had been on my curiosity radar for years.

A 57-acre property founded in 1894 by snowbirds from a spiritualist community in upstate New York, residents who practiced there had to pass mediumship exams. Was my mother guiding me here?

We'd never made any pacts about the afterlife, but my mother and I had long bonded over all things predictive. Recent hints of Mom had left me wanting more. What would she have to say about Florida?

As I barreled toward the Sunshine State, I wondered if Mom was leading me. Alive or dead, Mom hadn't ever expressed an opinion on Florida, but I wouldn't be on my way there if it weren't for her brother, my Uncle Tommy, with whom I'd couch-surfed in Tampa on my book tour. He'd shown me the condos. That had to be her guidance. *Right?*

I pulled over and searched on my phone for "mediums near me," and "open now." The woman I reached didn't mind if I brought Hartley, which was how I came to have an appointment later that same afternoon with the Reverend Suzanne.

Her house/office was a quaint white frame-style Victorian not far from the town center. Greeting me at the door, Suzanne wore a floral top, a skirt, and minimal jewelry. Normal enough for someone who trucked in dead people.

Pulling out a Tarot deck, Suzanne asked me to shuffle. Not wanting to influence the reading, I cleared my mind, determined to reveal as little as possible.

"I'm moving to Florida and wonder if it's the right next step."

But Rev. Suzanne wanted more.

"No, I don't have children."

And more.

"Divorced. His idea."

This was starting to grate.

"Nope, single."

Why all the romance, lady? I wanted her to talk to my mother so I could find out what she thought about this move. Not that I would be staying in Florida. What would she think about L.A.? In the interest of moving this along, I offered some intel.

"A few months ago, my mother died, and I was wondering—"

Only now, the Rev. Suzanne had lost interest in my contribution. "If you move to Florida," she cut me off mid-sentence, "you will always be alone."

For much of the decade since my divorce, I might well have run for my car and driven straight back to New York City. Instead, I drove onward toward my Florida condo, shaking my head along the way. I didn't need an intermediary to get in touch with my mother any more than I needed to find a home outside myself. I knew exactly who I was.

In a twist of cosmic irony, I did end up staying in Florida because there I met the man who would become my favorite husband. But that's an entirely separate story.

The price of happiness has been letting go of the things that cause misery. Simple as this choice sounds— who wouldn't pick bliss over unhappiness?— by making a bone-deep art of seeking my faults, I lost the ability to distinguish between the two. Finding my flaws was my quest yet achieving my goal made me anything but happy—each discovery was new reason for lament.

When I could see my imperfections with compassion, I found more to let go of. The ongoing task has been, with each new discovery, to start again without judgment. The only reason I know this is thanks to the teachers who didn't tell me what to think but how to think, with honesty, love, and always through the lens of grace.

ABOUT THE AUTHOR

L.L. Kirchner is an award-winning screenwriter and author of the best-selling memoir *American Lady Creature: (My) Change in the Middle East*, named one of Bustle's "11 Books to Battle the Blues." A book critic, essayist and reporter, Kirchner was once simultaneously the religion editor for an LGBTQ+ paper, dating columnist for an alt newsweekly, and bridal editor for a society rag. Her writing has appeared in Shondaland, The Rumpus, and The Washington Post among numerous others. Her short film was accepted into sixteen festivals and took top honors in three, and she's working on a pilot based on her second memoir, as well as a historical fiction novel. Since moving to Florida, she's become a guest host for the Home Shopping Network, and runs the monthly storytelling show, True Stories. She still lives with her beloved dog, Hartley, as well as favorite husband. His two grown children live nearby—Miss Lorena was right.

More at www.LLKirchner.com. Or for the less committed, on socials everywhere @llkirchner_.

ACKNOWLEDGEMENTS

My mom, dad, and sister were (and are) the contour of my world, and I've been helped by many friends along the way. Valerie, Debra, Jenny, Willy, Sophia, and Jane you know from these pages, and each person named within my story represents at least a dozen more to thank.

I'm also deeply indebted to my writing group, the Twenty-Third Street Salon, all of whom have made me a better writer. Then there are the life champions whose support and patience and early reads of my work have been crucial, my dear friends Eugenie Bondurant, Trish Collins, Laura Davis, Kate Evans, Christy Moceri, and Court Stroud. My gratitude extends as well to my editor and publisher extraordinaire, Diane Windsor. And I would be nowhere without my earliest writing cohort, Jennifer Bannan and Julie Albright. All of which is to say, though writing itself is a solitary pursuit, I've never found it lonely, and I am immensely grateful to have a life graced with kindred spirits such as these.

Most of all, for being my home, the shape of all good things in my life, my beloved, my Paul.

Made in the USA
Middletown, DE
31 October 2023